TIMBERHILL:

CHRONICLE OF A RESTORATION

by

Sibylla Brown

To Bill, whose encouragement, partnership, and unfailing support have made this endeavor so rewarding.

TABLE OF CONTENTS

ACKNOWLEDGEMENTS

RESTORING OUR LAND WOULD NEVER HAVE been possible without the guidance and patient support of the people who helped us. Bill Craig built our house, helped us with every prescribed burn, and taught us all we needed to learn about living in the country. Randy Goerndt was willing to break from traditional sawlog production and support savanna restoration. Rich Erke and the Decatur County Conservation Board supported our efforts. Dan and Vicki Fogle completed all timber stand improvement work using only handheld tools. Jim Munson and Pauline Drobney immediately recognized and supported the restoration potential of our land. Lois Tiffany was willing to answer any question no matter how stupid or how many times she had already answered it. Wayne Petersen taught us the importance of restoring the land's natural hydrology. Chris Bair found grant money to support the Timberhill landscape management study. Gerould Wilhelm and Laura Rericha confirmed the value of our efforts and gave us, mere enthusiastic amateurs, the courage to proceed.

Aerial photo of Timberhill, the red line indicating the property boundaries.

I.

A TIMBERHILL TOUR

IN 1985, WHEN MY HUSBAND, BILL, and I purchased land in south central Iowa, we had no idea that it was a rare oak savanna. We'd been living in Des Moines since 1963. With our children grown and Bill close to retirement, we entered a new phase in our life; we could live wherever we wanted. We traveled extensively looking for the perfect place. We immersed ourselves in Italian country life, food, and wine at a Tuscan estate. For several weeks we basked in the sunshine of Provence. We fell in love with the Florida Keys but couldn't imagine living there full-time. The stark beauty of the southwestern United States was appealing, yet no matter where we traveled, we realized that the *terroir* of Iowa suited us best. Nonetheless, we didn't want to continue to live in town. We decided to move to the country.

Our search for land took us farther and farther from the city until we discovered Woodland Township in Decatur County on the Iowa-Missouri border, seventy miles south of Des Moines, halfway between the Missouri and Mississippi Rivers in the Southern Iowa Drift Plain. In the half a million years since the last glaciers retreated from south central Iowa the upland glacial plain has undergone extensive erosion into a drainage pattern that looks like the branches of a tree. Ephemeral flow paths, creeks, and rivers have dissected the landscape into steeply rolling hills and valleys that branch off the ridgelines. Most of the creeks and rivers flow in a north-south direction. Traveling those directions, one can usually follow a ridge, but going from east to west, a traveler must cross a series of alternating ridges and valleys. Early settlers described travel in this direction as a "devil's washboard" (Howell and Smith 1915, 23).

The weathered soils that overlay the impervious clay till were too low in fertility for row crops, which could only be grown in the creek and river bottoms. As a result, wildflowers, native grasses, and sedges, remnants of pre-settlement plant diversity, had survived in the unplowed woodlands, the pastures, and even the roadside ditches.

Bill and I were compelled by the natural beauty of the land and the variety of landscapes we found—creeks with adjacent wetlands, riparian and upslope woodlands, and prairie remnants on the ridgetops and west-facing slopes. Although degraded, all contained elements of their unique ecological environments.

This is a photo of a wide-crowned oak tree, also known as "Wolf Tree."

The mature oak trees were the first thing we noticed about Timberhill. They were scattered throughout the woodlands from the north boundary along Pony Farm Road south to the old quarter-section line road, our south property line. They formed a canopy over the tractor trail that led uphill from Brush Creek, surrounded the ridgetop prairie, dotted the hillslopes, and etched the ravines that descended to Brush Creek.

Most of the land we purchased had not been farmed or pastured since the 1960s. Surrounded by water with Brush Creek to the north and east, the Weldon River to the south, and West Creek to the west, the property's only access was a tractor trail through the creek navigable only in dry weather. Before World War II, Brush Creek had been little more than a trickle that one could easily cross with a horse and buggy or motor vehicle. As the land became more settled and the US Army Corps of Engineers straightened and dredged the waterways, the creek cut deeper and deeper. Eventually it was too deep to keep the water gap fenced, and livestock grazing of the property was discontinued. Only the lower fields between Brush Creek and Pony Farm Road had been cultivated.

Timberhill comprises two hundred acres, which we purchased in sections. Our first purchase, in 1985, was a hundred twenty acres bordered by Brush Creek and Pony Farm Road; this included the North and East Savannas. In 1993 we began construction of a house on the ridgetop, a hundred feet above the road. To access the building site, we built a seventy-foot bridge across Brush Creek. From there the driveway follows the ridgeline winding up the steep hill through the North Savanna, which opens into a sunny meadow at the crest of the ridge. Surrounding the house and meadow, the land drops sharply to the east, west, and north in a succession of wooded hills and ravines. To the south, a horse trail used first by migrating Indians, later early settlers, follows the ridgeline into adjacent property.

The ridgetop meadow's soil was exhausted by early settlers, and it has taken years of management to reestablish a cover of Indian grass and little bluestem. Tall green milkweed, creamy gentian, and rough blazing star are also making a comeback. From the driveway in front of the house, the East Savanna trail follows a ridgeline east under widely spaced white oaks spread over an understory of little and big bluestem, June grass, sedges, and many colorful wildflowers. The trail leaves the ridgetop as it descends downhill to the Brush Creek bottom. Under a canopy of white oak, hickory, and black oak, woodland sunflower dominates the understory with occasional patches of wildflowers found only in high-quality remnant woodlands. Midway to the creek, the trail turns south, and the plant composition changes. Each spring, hundreds of wild hyacinth, bluebells, wild geranium, and bellwort cascade down the hillsides on either side of the trail. On the east-facing hillslopes across a ravine, one can see numerous bunches of broad, plaited leaves-this is false hellebore, a plant listed as threatened in Iowa.

At the creek bottom, oak and hickory give way to a riparian woodland of slippery elm, silver maple, hackberry, and basswood. In a good year, a spring crop of morel mushrooms fruits under the elm and silver maple trees. Continuing south, the trail returns uphill into oak and hickory woodland. Lousewort, well established on both sides of the trail, is moving downhill in an ever-widening circle. Nearing the top of the hill, the trail flattens out to a gradual upslope. For a short stretch, it joins a neighbor's road that used to run south to the Weldon River bridge, then reenters Timberhill through the south gate.

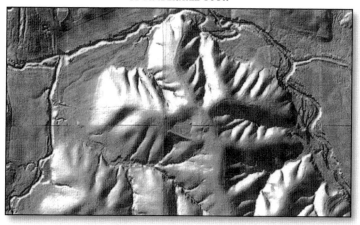

In this topographical map of Timberhill one can see the "devil's washboard" of steep hills and valleys encountered by the east west traveler.

Left from the gate, the south trail takes us into the West 40, purchased in 2001. This unit contributed two virgin prairie remnants, a wetland, and a white oak and bur oak savanna to the diversity of Timberhill. Walking west on the trail, one crosses the Decatur County "devil's washboard" of steep hills and valleys until the trail terminates at West Creek. When we purchased the West 40, we were surprised to find a high-quality prairie remnant on the west-facing slope above West Creek. Since it was completely surrounded by woodland, we named it Hidden Prairie. Each year our prescribed burns extend its perimeter as fire eradicates the scrub shingle oak and briars that hedged the prairie when we purchased it.

The trail ends at West Creek, a shallow sandy creek that separates the West 40 from the West Creek unit, purchased in 2004. Across the shallow, sandy creek, another trail runs north through the West Creek unit. The remnant wetland, sedge meadow, and active seeps in this unit contribute to the wide diversity of plants and wildlife that define the best of south central Iowa's varied habitat. We are continuing to restore wetland and virgin prairie in this unit. Considering its history of heavy grazing and its dense cover of eastern red cedar, we're surprised how fast it's recovering. Hairy mountain mint, slender mountain mint, and common mountain mint line a trail that turns north through sedge meadow and prairie. Six varieties of milkweed stagger their bloom from June into September, making this a haven for butterflies. We have even seen rare regal fritillaries nectaring on butterfly milkweed in the prairie remnants.

A low-water crossing through the creek returns the trail to the West 40. After the creek it turns south through the West 40 bottom. In the section between the trail and the creek, we are slowly making progress restoring the wetland under a tangle of multiflora rose and heavy brush. We have yet to see fire move through the entire tract, but each prescribed burn transforms more of this wilderness. So far it has restored a complex of long-awned tussock sedge, prairie cord grass, and patches of bottle gentian and Indian grass. Experience has taught us to recognize overstocked savanna and prairie remnants, but we don't know how to classify this tract. All we know is that it's some kind of wetland.

The trail continues south into elm and river birch woodland. Pileated woodpeckers have torn through the bark of several river birch, exposing large sections of heartwood. Fresh woodchips around the base of the trees are evidence of their continual excavations. The hillside south of the trail is a remnant bur oak and white oak savanna. To the north the trail separates another prairie remnant from the hickory grove. It terminates in the ridgetop meadow just west of the house.

Bill and I had no plans to farm our land. But we did want to take care of it. Most immediately, between the briars and heavy woody midstory, it was impossible to walk through the woods in summer without a machete. Working with Iowa Department of Natural Resources district forester Randy Goerndt, we began timber stand improvement, thinning ten to fifteen acres of woodland per year starting in 1993. But we were uncertain of what else we should do.

In 1994, the summer after we moved into our new house at the farm, US Fish and Wildlife Service Private Lands coordinator for Iowa Jim Munson brought biologist Pauline Drobney to Timberhill. Jim was a patient in Bill's dental practice. Knowing that Jim had specific knowledge about restoring native lands, Bill had sought his advice. Their discussions piqued Jim's interest, and they arranged a visit to Timberhill. Pauline accompanied Jim. Pauline had attended an oak savanna conference the previous year, and she immediately recognized that our land was a rare oak savanna remnant.

As we toured the woodlands with her, Pauline took out paper and pencil and began scribbling names of plants, "Scaly blazing star, wild hyacinth, and purple milkweed, these are all high savanna indicators," she said. According to her, thinning the timber wasn't enough to restore the oak savanna. She told me we would have to implement prescribed fire. Not only would fire control the midstory, but it would also release plants that had been suppressed by lack of sunlight and fire.

Neither Bill nor I had any experience or training in ecological restoration. To acquaint myself with the subject, I read everything I could find regarding oak savanna and how to restore it. I wanted to believe what Pauline had told me, that our woodland was a rare habitat and that continued thinning and prescribed fire would restore the savanna. But according to Victoria Nuzzo's 1985 survey of Midwest oak savanna, Iowa's only savanna remnants were found in the Loess Hills, the Little Sioux River drainage system in northwest Iowa, and the driftless region of northeast Iowa. There was no mention of south central Iowa (Nuzzo 1986).

It was furthermore assumed that restoration of the herbaceous layer could be achieved only by seeding savanna indicator species. "Evidence consistently indicates that soil seed bank persistence is poor for sites that have been degraded for longer than a few decades and for forest/woodland species in general" (Brudvig and Mabry 2008, 291–292).

I didn't want to seed, because I didn't know what belonged where. Yellow giant hyssop, for example, was included on all the savanna indicator plant lists, but where in our two hundred acres of woodland and prairie did it belong? Also, instinct told me that seeding of species not in the Timberhill seed bank might produce unintended consequences. Better to settle for whatever suppressed plants were released by fire and increased sunlight. (As it turned out, I eventually found yellow giant hyssop in the North Savanna and West 40.)

It was serendipity that friends brought botanist Gerould Wilhelm to Timberhill in June 2003. On that visit he noted 206 native plant species, a high number for a single visit. (He is usually gratified to note 180 species in a single survey of a high-quality remnant.) I well remember that day and his positive response to Timberhill. Three months later he returned with biologist Laura Rericha who recorded 22 native ant species, a high number in a single plant community. Between the two of them, they could name every plant, every bird, and every insect they found at Timberhill. I had been looking for someone to help guide our restoration, to help me understand the processes that were evolving; Laura and Gerould were the experts I was looking for. They could assess what we had done and guide our future management.

In 2005, Chris Bair at the Iowa Valley Resource Conservation and Development found funding for a grant so that Laura and Gerould could assess Timberhill management (Wilhelm and Rericha 2007). Their study validated our efforts; since then Bill and I have been able to proceed with more confidence.

By trial and error, following Randy Goerndt's and Laura and Gerould's advice and our own instincts, this restoration succeeded well beyond our expectations. The purpose of this book is not to describe a specific management program that applies to all savanna restorations. It is to share the story of one restoration. We have learned that restoration is not about following a set of rules but about listening to the land and observing the response of plants and animals to the management applied. This book shares what worked for us, as nearly twenty years of woodland management by thinning and prescribed fire stimulated the restoration of this ecosystem.

2.

WHAT IS AN OAK SAVANNA?

BEFORE THE PLOW, THIRTY MILLION ACRES of open oak woodlands formed the transition between the eastern deciduous forest and the tallgrass prairie. This landscape of widely spaced oak trees that spread over an understory of wildflowers, sedges, and grasses stretched from Minnesota and Wisconsin south to the Texas Hill country in a shifting mosaic of prairie, wetland, woodland, and savanna. It was a broad transition zone that varied due to the frequency and intensity of fire and drought. After European settlement, what wasn't converted to farmland became dense forest. Only a few intact remnants remain (Nuzzo 1986).

Midwest oak savannas evolved from eight thousand to thirty-five hundred years ago after the retreat of the last glaciers when Amerindians began burning the land (Anderson, Fralish, and Baskin 1999). The oral tradition of many tribes contains versions of a legend in which Coyote brought fire to the people. The Paiute version is believed to date back ten to fifteen thousand years, to the retreat of the Wisconsin Ice Sheet. According to the legend, the people had no fire, were cold, and were forced to eat their food raw. The only fire was on top of a mountain guarded day and night by three shamans. Coyote and his friends plotted to steal fire from the shamans. They lulled the shamans to sleep and then "Coyote grabbed the last burning ember from the fire. The shamans chased him, but as he ran through the landscape, he tossed the ember to his allies in a relay race around the world. And as Coyote, Eagle, Bull, Hare, and others ran, light entered each land, and the great ice melted" (Cayete 2000, 167).

In the Karok version, fire ended up in Wood, where Coyote demonstrated to the people how to get fire out of Wood. He rubbed two dry sticks together until sparks ignited dry moss, wood chips, and small twigs (First People website).

Amerindians burned the land annually, usually in late fall after the first hard frost (Stewart 2002). Fire stimulated growth of the plants that they used for food, medicine, dyes, and fibers for basketry and weaving. Fire was also an important tool for game management. Fire was used to drive wild game, and deer. Other woodland prey were easier to track and shoot in the open woodland after fire. Another aboriginal practice was to leave an unburned area; deer were drawn to the grass surrounded by scorched land, where they were easily dispatched.

Frequent fire maintained the open woodlands by top-killing the numerous woody sprouts and grubs in the understory. Fire did not damage the roots which rapidly regrew into trees after European settlement. Within twenty to forty years, the savanna remnants succeeded to closed oak canopy forests with dense midstories of invasive brush and pole timber (Curtis 1959). Without fire, the natural succession from oak-dominated woodlands to mixed overstocked forests with heavy midstory trees depleted the biodiversity of oak savanna remnants. They evolved into species-poor forests with sparse understory plants. What didn't succeed to closed forest has been largely destroyed by clearing, plowing, or overgrazing.

European settlers suppressed fire to increase the extent and value of their woodlots and forests. They believed that fire destroyed timber (Pyne 1982). Just the opposite is true of oak savannas. Fire is essential to their ecology. The thick bark and deep roots of white and bur oaks, the dominant Midwest savanna trees, make them fire-resistant. Fire will only destroy the invasives and excess growth that don't belong.

This is a photo of a wolf tree in an overstocked savanna.
The lower branches died after the understory filled in.

In general, savanna can be defined as a fire-dependent landscape with scattered trees that spread over a diverse understory of grasses, sedges, and wildflowers. From the bur oak savannas of Minnesota to the oak woodlands of the Texas hill country, there are many variations in the savanna transition zone. Oak and pine communities of the Ozark plateaus and post oak and blackjack oak savannas that extend from southern Kansas into Texas are examples (Anderson, Fralish, and Baskin 1999).

Oaks, which have a disproportionate effect on the ecosystem relative to their biomass, are the ecologically dominant species in this habitat. Oaks provide more habitat than any other native tree (Tallamy 2009): 96 animal species (Fralish 2004), 534 butterfly and moth species, and a diverse ground layer of wildflowers, grasses, and sedges. If their habitat is not maintained, there will not be enough trees to sustain oak dominance as existing trees age and die. The overstocked remnants will provide inadequate sunlight to sustain oak regeneration (Randy Goerndt, personal communication 1993). The acorns may germinate but cannot mature. With no replacement trees to perpetuate the oak habitat, mature oaks will be replaced by eastern red cedar, slippery elm, American elm, and maple.

Decline of this ecosystem severely affects avian populations of species such as the redheaded woodpecker, which can only thrive and breed successfully in open woodlands with mature and standing dead oak trees (Sibley 2001). The mosaic of grassland, savanna, and successional scrub is also the preferred habitat of a suite of birds that include the Baltimore oriole and the eastern kingbird. These open-country species are also in serious decline (Brawn 1998).

Sedge growing in degraded savanna

Recent efforts have shown that many thousands of acres of overgrown woodlands are actually savanna remnants (McCarty 1998). Unlike the many Midwest prairies that have been completely lost to agriculture or development, savanna remnants can be restored. Woodlands that have not been plowed or seeded with nonnative pasture grasses are merely degraded and will sustain portions of their native plant diversity. All they require to release the suppressed plants is fire and the sunlight that follows when the canopy is opened. Depending on previous land use such as grazing, actively managing these systems can restore the oak dominance and a diverse understory of wildflowers, grasses, and sedges in as little as three years. Deeply shaded and highly degraded woodlands may take much longer, but they too can recover.

Although each piece of land has its own set of plants, some specifics may identify savanna remnants. One should first look for woodlands with unevenly aged trees. The presence of wolf trees (oak trees with wide crowns), whose lower branches have died from lack of sunlight, is a strong indicator of a savanna remnant. The dead lower branches indicate that the trees had more space to grow before they were surrounded by pole timber.

Grasslike sedge plants in this photo of an overstocked woodland indicate a degraded savanna with high potential for restoration.

Lists of savanna indicator species that ecologists believe once comprised the understory plants are often used to assess whether a woodland is a degraded savanna (Pruka 1994). However, since no inventories of pre-settlement savannas exist, we can only guess which plants grew where or how this system originally functioned (Nuzzo 1986). What is certain is that the understory plants consisted of a mix of native prairie and woodland species, particularly sedges, legumes, and late-season blooming grasses such as bottlebrush grass and wild rye (Curtis 1959). I have also observed that the presence of purple milkweed at the woodland border probably indicates a savanna remnant.

Purple milkweed blooming at a woodland border strongly indicates that the woodland is savanna remnant.

When we purchased it Bill and I didn't know that Timberhill was a rare oak savanna remnant. To our eyes, the only difference between our land and most contemporary woodlands was the number of wolf trees. We now know that Timberhill could easily have been identified as a savanna remnant. Despite years of neglect, extensive timber harvest, and a history of heavy grazing, Timberhill still retained some of the varied woodland and prairie structure. In the sharply dissected landscape were grassland ridgetops surrounded by mature oaks, their lower branches grazing the prairie grasses and wildflowers. Prairie openings with warm-season grasses and wildflowers interrupted the woodlands. Still hanging on in the sun-bereft woodlands were patches of pen sedge, woodland sunflower, and pointed tick trefoil. In late summer we could find sky-blue aster where sunlight penetrated the canopy. Even some of the songbirds had survived the habitat degradation. On a morning walk before we began restoration, we flushed a flock of eastern bluebirds feasting on seeds of little blue stem.

This Timberhill ridgetop prairie surrounded by mature white oaks is typical of the mosaic of woodland and prairie that comprise southern Iowa oak savannas.

There are many who believe that one should let nature take its course in Midwest temperate woodlands, that they are best left alone. They believe that the forces of nature determine a natural succession that will eventually result in a stable community. The final stage of this process may result in an overstocked, species-poor forest, but it will be pure. They would have us put fences around remnant woodlands, keep people out, and let natural succession take its course.

But they are forgetting that we have denied these woodlands the pre-settlement fires that controlled the understory, and that the few remaining remnants are so fragmented they can no longer support the bison and elk whose grazing regulated plant composition. Without human intervention, the natural succession from grassland to woody shrubs to oak and hickory will result in an overstocked timber bereft of floristic (plant) diversity. In these dense, dark woodlands, there is not enough understory vegetation to control erosion, hold the soil, or keep seeds from washing away with every rainfall. Each year the ravines will continue to cut more deeply into the hillsides, further degrading the land. Natural springs and seeps will no longer issue a constant source of groundwater to sustain wild orchids and other rare perennials. Active management with prescribed fire and timber stand improvement, however, can restore a fully functioning savanna ecosystem in as little as three years. Pre-settlement conditions may never be duplicated, but the restored woodland will function as an oak savanna.

3.

WHERE DOES THE PRAIRIE END

AND THE SAVANNA BEGIN?

"Where does the prairie end and the savanna begin?" I asked. District forester Randy Goerndt and I were standing in the East Savanna at the border between the woodland and the prairie opening south of the house. Instead of a sharp line separating the prairie from the woodland, scattered shingle oaks, their lower branches dead or dying, made the transition between the woodland and prairie. To my eye, the shingle oaks looked like they were intruders on the prairie opening. I didn't think they belonged but wanted an expert opinion before cutting them down.

"You take those trees out and you'll have a prairie," he replied, indicating the shingle oaks between the woodland and the South Meadow. That wasn't the answer I was looking for. I wanted to know exactly what should be prairie, what savanna, and what open woodland. In the mosaic of woodland and prairie openings that comprised Timberhill, how could I tell where the prairie should end and the savanna begin? How would I know if we had thinned enough trees in the woodland? What plants should comprise the understory? Being told that a savanna was a prairie with trees didn't answer these questions.

Research into a specific land's history provides some answers to these questions. Primary sources that record the historical conditions of a particular property are available to most landowners. They include the original General Land Office (GLO) survey notes, United States Department of Agriculture (USDA) aerial photos, oral history passed down through families of early settlers, and data compiled by early botanists.

The General Land Office survey notes describe the land surveyed by the crews. In Iowa these surveys were compiled in the mid-nineteenth century. Before the government could sell land to pioneers, each square mile of the frontier had to be surveyed. The survey crew may have been the first Euro-Americans to walk the land. After completion, the surveyor's notes were turned over to the Land Office. Still available, they list the location of all trees, creeks, and rivers the surveyor encountered when he walked his square-mile grid. The surveyor also noted the soil type and whether the land was woodland or prairie. The vast government land holdings were divided into six square-mile townships that were subdivided into square-mile sections. At the section and quarter section corners, he listed the distance, diameter, and direction of bearing tree species. Tree species and undergrowth he encountered along the section line were also listed in order of dominance (Wisconsin Board of Commissioners of Public Lands).

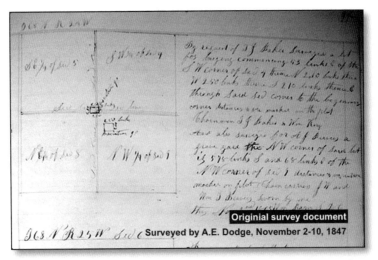

Original survey document
Surveyed by A.E. Dodge, November 2-10, 1847

Original survey notes for Woodland Township, Decatur County, Iowa.[

I found a copy of the Decatur County survey notes at the county engineer's office. Timberhill was surveyed in November 1847. Walking a square-mile grid, the survey crew went west along what is now our north property line. The surveyor's notes indicate that the land was elm woodland. They crossed Brush Creek at approximately the same location where it now flows under Pony Farm Road, although it is currently much deeper and wider. Part of this bottomland still contains elm-dominated woodlands, but most of it has been converted to crop fields.

At the corner between sections 5 and 6, Woodland Township, the crew turned south and walked the line between our east and west units. They crossed another creek just south of the Woodland Township north boundary. That creek is also still in the same approximate location. After the creek they walked uphill through white oak, black oak, and hickory timber with "oak and hazle undergrowth." The soil was "second rate." Oak and hickory timber still extends south through sections 5 and 6 but at a much higher stocking. When the crew walked that line, they listed no trees until they noted two white oaks near the quarter-section corner. Were they to walk that line now, they would have to record countless black oaks and white oaks.

When the General Land Office survey crew walked south between sections 5 and 6 (fence line), Woodland Township, they did not record a single tree until they reached the quarter-section corner. This photo shows many trees along that line at the present time.

USDA aerial photos are another valuable land history source. Available for every county beginning around 1940, they record a bird's-eye view of property changes. They can be found at the county USDA office and the Iowa Geographic Map Server website. The earliest aerials are located at the USDA office. More recent photos, an 1800s historic vegetation map based on the GLO survey notes, and topographic maps are available on the Iowa Geographic Map Server site. The Timberhill 1941 aerial photo shows an open woodland of widely spaced canopy trees and larger prairie openings. The only fully stocked timber was in the southeast corner. Prairie openings extended like fingers from the ridgetop into the woodland. One can also make out the pioneer horse trail that led north from adjacent property through the South Meadow, then downhill to Brush Creek.

1941 USDA aerial photo of Timberhill

In 1941 the West 40 was all prairie or pasture except for a small remnant oak savanna. When we purchased this unit the prairie was almost completely overgrown with eastern red cedar, honey locust, and elm trees. Only two small prairie openings, surrounded by the nearly impassable thickets of weed trees, had survived the neglect. Bottle gentian and other rare wildflowers, indicators of what had been, were hanging on in the two remnants. The savanna remnant was so overgrown it was barely recognizable. The hickory grove just west of the line between sections 5 and 6, a dense canopy of pole timber in 2001, had been only brush.

West 40 prairie remnant before restoration,
infested with red cedar and other weed trees.

23

In the 1941 West Creek unit photo, one can still make out the spring that supplied water for the early settler's homestead. Imprints of a wagon trail that led from a quarter-section line road along the south property line to the pioneer spring are still discernible. The previous owner had acquired a tractor in 1938. He plowed a crop field on the creek bottom and seeded a ridgetop to pasture. The rest was virgin prairie and wetland. When we purchased it in 2004, there were two corn fields, one on the creek bottom, the other on a hillside above the creek. The cover of eastern red cedar, shingle oak, honey locust, and elm trees was so dense over the rest that it was hard to tell what was what. A deep erosional run that cut this unit in half flowed into a large puddle of willows. Honey locusts, their large trunks covered with stinging needles, covered the ground along West Creek.

Conversations with neighbors who were descendants of the original settlers provided us with the most valuable information. One neighbor told us that his grandmother had witnessed a fire that burned through Timberhill around 1900. It burned through the prairie and woodland, stopping only when it reached Brush Creek.

The land had been heavily grazed. From May through late fall, fifteen head of cattle grazed the land in section 5 for thirty years prior to 1967. Our neighbor Doyle Butcher, who used to hunt the West 40, told us that the woodland west of the house was "pretty well open. You could see pretty much all over this. It's really grown up since they took the cattle out. They hit this pretty hard." When he hunted, he could see West Creek from the border of the hickory grove at the east boundary of this unit. Even after we cut the weed trees and thinned the rest, it was impossible to see West Creek from this vantage point.

Recent USDA aerial photo with GLO entries shows
how much woodlands have filled in since 1941.

Another neighbor, Miles Leeper's, great uncle had settled the West 40 and West Creek units. Describing the land, Miles told me, "All those hills were prairie. My uncle said even on land that had trees, it was pretty well open. Under the trees were bluestem and lots of wildflowers. My dad said Uncle told my grandfather that when they came here, there weren't many trees as such. It was prairie every place, even under the trees. The land when they came here was really productive, but it didn't take long with the rains and erosion, to lose the topsoil."

The hickory grove in the West 40 had been a horse pasture, "mostly native grass," until the owners bought a tractor in 1938, replacing the need for horses. When we purchased the property, a dense stand of hickory had replaced the horse pasture.

I asked Miles about the wildflowers. Did he remember seeing any?

"Oh, gosh yes, there used to be all kinds of wildflowers. I don't remember the names. In fact it was all just about any wildflower that grew. They were abundant because it was in pasture and it wasn't plowed. They'll regenerate themselves if they have a chance. Surprising how long the seed will last. On land that's been turned back to pasture, they'll be back in ten years. And you'll see flowers that you never saw in there before."

Data collected by early botanists has been another valuable resource. T. J. Fitzpatrick and his wife, Mary Frances Linder Fitzpatrick, compiled surveys of southern Iowa plants between 1892 and 1898. Two papers published in the Iowa Academy of Science bulletin list all the plants they discovered. These papers also describe the soil, habitat, and location of each species.

In a history of Decatur County, the Fitzpatricks' article "Forest Trees and Shrubs of Decatur County," describes Decatur County as "essentially an expanse of prairie with narrow sinuous belts of timber stretched along Grand River and its tributaries. Unbroken prairie is being slowly occupied by forests." This paper includes a list of all oak species found in the county. All Timberhill species, white oak, shingle oak, bur oak, chinquapin oak, red oak, and black oak are listed except two hybrids: Bebb's oak and Hawkin's oak (Howell and Smith 1915).

Regarding white oak, Fitzpatrick states, "White oak, hard maple, and other trees of like character are too few in number to be of consequence"(Howell and Smith 1915, 271). According to Fitzpatrick, shingle oak, the tree that I thought had intruded in our prairie opening, was found only in poorly managed woodland or abandoned pasturelands. The article "Native Oak Groves of Iowa," also by the Fitzpatricks, bemoans the dearth of large trees. They did, however, note numerous large tree stumps that were a record of mature trees harvested to provide fuel, lumber, and fence posts (Fitzpatrick and Fitzpatrick 1901).

"Prairie Openings in the Forest" by Bohumil Shimek, another early Iowa naturalist, lists plants found in "treeless openings in otherwise forested areas" that distinctly contrast with typical plants of timbered areas. Plants in the oak openings are "invariably of the same general prairie type." The size of these openings is "exceedingly variable in extent," sometimes only "a few square rods." The prairie openings and forest "blend with a scant sprinkling of trees, usually stunted hardwood species such as oaks." Shimek found these openings on "the very tops of ridges or on southwesterly slopes." Many species found in Timberhill savanna are among those collected in the prairie openings by Shimek (Shimek 1910).

More recent botanical information is found in Theodore Van Bruggen's PhD dissertation, "The Flora of South Central Iowa," which describes distinctive plant communities and lists the common plants he collected in each community. "Dry upland woods" and "dry, sandy open woods" included two sites he surveyed in Decatur County. Both of these sites remain unmanaged natural areas, although now severely overgrown. A walk through each demonstrates how native plant diversity declines without light and fire (Van Bruggen 1958).

The land history documents were like pieces of a puzzle. They helped us fit together a picture of how Timberhill must have looked in 1847 along with some of the plants that probably comprised the understory. It was encouraging to learn that many of those plants had endured despite having been subjected to heavy grazing, extensive timber harvest, and fire suppression. Although it would probably not be enough to restore its original plant diversity, we chose to continue to manage our land only with prescribed fire and timber stand improvement.

Some plants were forever lost due to heavy grazing and fire suppression. We accepted that it was unlikely we could replicate the understory plant diversity to 1847 conditions (Gerould Wilhelm, personal communication 2005). From Miles we had also learned that it was likely that management would stimulate plants from the seed bank. Rather than try to replace what was lost, our goal became to restore a fully functioning ecosystem that would continue to evolve.

Even after thinning, Timberhill supported many more trees than were recorded in the General Land Office survey and the Fitzpatrick papers. We did not interpret that as a mandate to do more thinning. As long as there was enough ambient light to support a diverse understory, we saw no need to cut more trees. Natural forces will continue to open the canopy as each year some trees are lost to disease, high winds, and fungal infection. The shingle oaks in the transition between the South Meadow and surrounding woodland are a good example. As proof that fire eliminates what doesn't belong, they are all dying; sedges and grasses restored by fire hold more moisture in the soil than these trees can tolerate, which has made them susceptible to honey fungus infection.

Discovering the story of our land had given us a deeper understanding of its unique character. It provided a context in which to make decisions regarding its restoration and strengthened our resolve to continue managing only with fire and timber stand improvement. We trusted that nature and time would do the rest.

4.

FORESTRY 101

IN 1993 WE BEGAN RESTORATION BY obtaining an assessment of our woodlands from a professional forester. Creating a management plan based on specific goals was the next step. With woodlands of different densities, trees of different ages, and prairie openings, our plan divided the property into five units: North Savanna, East Savanna, West Woodland, a riparian area along Brush Creek, and the South Meadow. After we purchased the West 40 and West Creek, each became a separate unit. Management recommendations were different for each. Not only did they differ in tree age and density, but the weedy midstory trees varied, with ironwood and prickly ash dominant in some and elm, eastern red cedar, and honey locust in others. Timber stand improvement—the thinning of the overstocked woodlands—was the final step.

Like many woodland owners, Bill and I lacked the specific woodland management knowledge to properly assess our site. We couldn't even distinguish between the various species of oak, much less identify any of the other trees. Our first step, therefore, was to consult the district forester. Iowa has a district forester for each of its twelve forestry districts. District foresters are trained to assess a woodland and assist the landowner in managing his or her woodland according to the landowner's goal. The forester can inventory the trees, spot any problems, and then prescribe a management plan that fits the landowner's needs. Working with a forester will also assist the landowner in making informed choices. He or she can determine a site's potential for restoration and recommend a timber stand improvement contractor. Cost-share funding is often available for contractor expenses.

The first thing forester Randy Goerndt asked us was what we wanted to do with our woodland. Did we want to manage it for timber production or improve the habitat for wildlife and recreation? We weren't sure how to answer that question. All we were certain of was that we wanted to be able to walk through the woods and save the big oak trees.

But Randy needed more specific goals in order to write a woodland stewardship plan. This was required if we wanted to qualify our project for cost-share that provided partial reimbursement for paying a timber contractor. Furthermore, the plan had to fit into a category prescribed by the Iowa Department of Forestry. Savanna restoration wasn't one of the prescribed categories when we began in 1993. However, various wildlife-habitat and recreation-management plans were available. Therefore, the stated goal of the 1993 plan was "to improve the stand for long-term wildlife benefits including the sustained production of oak-hickory wildlife mast (nuts)." The 1994 plan stipulated wildlife habitat enhancement "to improve the overall health and vigor of the stand for the sustained production of all forest benefits with special emphasis on wildlife habitat improvement for deer and turkeys." The 1996 plan for the North Savanna was "to improve the capability of the woodland to reproduce desirable oak tree seedlings." It wasn't until 2002 when we began managing the West 40 that the stated goal became savanna restoration.

Wolf tree in severely overstocked West 40
savanna remnant before restoration

Overall, according to Randy, our woodland was severely over-stocked and needed thinning. He suggested that our primary goal be to restore oak vigor and regeneration. The understory in our over-stocked woodlands was too shaded for oak regeneration. The acorns germinated, but they required 10 to 25 percent ambient sunlight for continued growth, and as mature trees died, there were no young oaks to replace them.

Furthermore, we couldn't manage for sawlog production if we wanted to save the mature oaks. They had no commercial value because of their short trunks. We could use them as seed source for natural reproduction, but they would have to be harvested when the next-generation trees were four feet high. The veteran trees also took up too much space for a forestry production stand.

The North Savanna was obviously an overgrown savanna. It was composed primarily of scattered mature white oaks with large spreading crowns over short thick trunks. Mixed grasses and an occasional native wildflower comprised the understory. The dead lower branches that extended over the ground indicated that the white oaks had once had little or no competition. The lower branches had died from lack of adequate sunlight. There was too much competition from the dense midstory bitternut and shagbark hickory, eastern red cedar, and prickly ash; they blocked sun from all but the upper crowns of the canopy trees.

Randy explained that timber stand improvement in such an overstocked savanna required only clearing the midstory and cutting or girdling badly deformed trees. This prepared the area for oak regeneration by giving all crop trees optimum room, light, and access to water and essential nutrients. It would increase mast production at higher sustained levels, providing plentiful seed for oak regeneration and food for wildlife. The added sunlight would also stimulate the understory wildflowers and grasses.

The mix of mature oaks and pole timber in the East Savanna required different management. This white, red, and black oak woodland had a much heavier stocking than the north savanna. The first priority was to weed out the understory by controlling the ironwood. This would allow oak seedlings to become established. We chose to favor the white oak development because of its long life and high value as a food source for birds, wild turkey, and deer (Stein, Binion, and Aciavetti 2003). But its stocking was too sparse. Randy told us that we would have to leave some red and black oak as well as some hickories to achieve an adequately stocked woodland. Since red oak is highly susceptible to oak wilt, he anticipated high mortality from this aggressive disease. He recommended a denser stocking to compensate for the anticipated tree loss.

Where the dominant trees were all approximately the same height, he recommended that we save trees with the best potential for crown expansion: straight with minimal forking, healthy and vigorous in dominant canopy positions, and over twenty-five feet tall. Selective thinning around the best-formed oak and hickory trees would promote crown expansion and larger diameters at an earlier age. Giving each tree ten to fifteen feet of open space on all sides would increase mast production earlier and at higher sustained levels.

Girdled tree deteriorates slowly,
providing wildlife habitat for many years

The most difficult thing to accept about woodland management is that you have to cut down trees to improve the woodland. In each unit, Randy selected the best-formed trees as crop trees. All other trees with crowns that touched or overtopped the canopies of crop trees were felled or girdled. That included trees that were not good seed trees as well as excessively crooked, deformed, or rotten trees. Girdling was used when a tree could not be felled without injuring a tree marked to be saved. Girdling kills a standing tree by interrupting the flow of sap between the roots and the crown of the tree. A groove one and a half inches deep is cut into the trunk, completely encircling the tree. Such trees deteriorate very slowly and provide habitat for many years to come.

Randy did not recommend any timber stand improvement in the woodland that extends west from the ridgetop meadow to the boundary between sections 5 and 6. It was "adequately stocked" with pole-and small sawlog-size white oaks and "required no work."

The West 40 unit when we purchased it in 2001 was mixed upland oak-hickory woodland and degraded savanna. The woodland was overstocked with pole-size white oak, black oak, shagbark hickory, shingle oak, and bur oak. Here Randy recommended that we release the crowded oaks and hickories from competing tree competition by spacing them forty feet apart. In the degraded white oak and bur oak savanna remnant, Randy recommended that we remove the entire woody understory under the crowns of the mature trees and "maintain a management regime by periodic controlled burning." By this time Bill and I had enough experience to know the value of prescribed fire, and we burned this unit before doing any thinning.

West 40 savanna remnant right after thinning

West 40 savanna remnant nine years after beginning restoration

The West Creek unit was completely different from the other units. The only large trees were weed trees: large honey locusts along the creek and uphill stands of eastern red cedars that completely obscured the prairie underneath. There was also a crop field that had been farmed since 1946. According to Randy, there was no woodland worth saving in this unit; he said it should all be prairie. This presented such a daunting challenge that we divided the work into manageable tasks. The first year, 2005, we began prescribed burns, followed by the removal of invasive trees from the prairie remnant above the old crop field. In 2006 we took the crop field out of production and seeded it with seed collected from the prairie remnant. That year our timber contractor, Dan Fogle, girdled all the honey locusts. The third year Dan returned to cut down all the remaining eastern red cedars and shingle oaks. Restoring this unit continues to be an ongoing project. Like the wetland across the creek, we're not certain what is prairie, what wetland.

Only living trees were cut down. Dead trees were left standing as redheaded and pileated woodpecker habitat. These species excavate a new nest cavity each year. After they abandon their nests, the excavations become habitat for other wildlife.

Only living trees are cut down.
Dead trees such as this are left for wildlife habitat.

Various tools and equipment may be used for timber stand improvement. Skid loaders, small engine powered machines with lift arms that attach to heavy heavy-duty scissor-like tree shears are often recommended for clearing thick brush and trees up to twelve inches in diameter. Attached to the front end of the machine, tree shears cut trees and brush to within one inch of the ground. Heavier-duty chopper mulchers clear and mulch small trees up to eight inches in diameter.

We didn't use either. We were hesitant to use any equipment that would compact the soil. Shredded wood chips from a chipper shredder can hold moisture that prevents prescribed fire from moving freely through a woodland. Dan and Vicki Fogle did all the work at Timberhill with hand-held equipment. Working through ten to fifteen acres per year, they used only chain saws and a hand-held brush cutter.

Most landowners want to clear their woodlands of downed wood. They cut it up for firewood or haul it away. We cut up some of the downed trees for firewood but left the rest on the ground. Downed trees provide browse and groundcover for wildlife. They also shield oak sprouts from deer predation. By the time the sprouts are tall enough to reach above the cover, they will be too mature to suit a deer's palate.

Dryad's saddle decomposer mushrooms

Deadwood includes living veteran trees with cavities and large canopies for perching and nesting, standing dead tree trunks, and downed logs. As deadwood breaks down, it provides habitat for many organisms and supports a large and complex food chain. Decomposer fungi begin the process. They release enzymes that break down the cellulose and lignin in the wood. This process converts organic nutrients into their inorganic forms. Some of these nutrients leach into the soil, where they become available to the plants (Dudley, Equilibrium, and Vallaurt 2004).

Insects inhabiting deadwood are the preferred food of woodpeckers. This log is being excavated by a pileated woodpecker.

The decomposition process also creates microhabitats for numerous invertebrates and their larvae. Some invertebrates even lay their eggs in the decomposer fungi. The insects and larvae inhabiting deadwood are the preferred food of woodpeckers and other cavity-nesting birds that are largely dependent on dead wood for both food and nesting sites. Clearing away deadwood greatly decreases the wildlife diversity of a woodland.

In the East Savanna, our first thinning was very conservative. Since we weren't certain how many trees to leave, we chose to err on the side of caution. Once a hundred-year-old tree is cut down, it can't be replaced. We knew that the understory plants needed sunlight but didn't know how much. The only way to determine the right canopy density was to watch the plants. Because of the nature of oak trees, some sunlight always penetrates the canopy. Light filters through the oak leaves as the sun moves across the sky, giving each plant a dose of dappled sunlight. It took ten years to know if enough of this dappled sunlight was reaching the ground. We knew that we could always do a second thinning if needed. Therefore, the first thinning consisted only of clearing the understory and cutting down trees that interfered with the crop trees.

We incorporated our own management plan with the woodland stewardship plan. This included an analysis of each site's existing plant communities, its exotic species, and any problems we found. Exotics were not a problem except on ground that had been disturbed by house and driveway construction. However, all units had problems with erosion. To begin with, our focus would be to control erosion and restore the understory. As we learned more about the restoration process, we knew we could reevaluate our goals.

In 1999, after timber stand improvement was completed, Timberhill had various canopy densities, from very open stocking to over 60 percent canopy density. The lightest stocking was on the East Savanna ridgetop, a site that is highly susceptible to lightning strikes. Several trees have been struck and killed since we purchased the land. Here we observed the highest diversity of understory plants, with many species of wildflowers, thick swards of warm-season grasses, and numerous sedges. South of there, under a denser canopy, plant diversity was much lower. Only the sunny woodland borders had high plant diversity. In 2003 and 2004, we chose to do a second thinning in the more heavily stocked East Savanna. It took only three years for many more flowering plants to become established there.

5.

PRESCRIBED FIRE AT TIMBERHILL

THE 1993 WOODLAND MANAGEMENT PLAN SUBMITTED by forester Randy Goerndt included a section entitled "General Practice Requirements." Item 2 stipulated that "the treated area be protected from fire." Eight years later, the stewardship plan he wrote for the West 40 unit stated, "prescribed burning of the savanna understory is recommended each year for at least the first five years following treatment to effectively control unwanted woody plant competition and promote native ground plant diversity." What had happened between 1993 and 2002 to convince Randy to recommend prescribed burns as part of savanna restoration? What had happened to convince us that he was right?

We had learned that oak savanna is a fire-dependent habitat and that fire is essential to the woodland ecology. In other words, you can't restore savanna without fire. Dangerous and destructive as it can be, fire becomes a creative, cleansing force in savanna restoration. Annual low-intensity woodland fires release nutrients into the soil, control the midstory, stimulate reproduction of grasses, sedges, and forbs, and remove surface litter to open sites for seed germination. What most impressed our forester was the extent to which fire stimulated acorn germination. Thousands of oak sprouts appeared each spring.

Like most people, Randy believed that fire should be kept out of woodlands. Foresters are trained to manage woodlands for maximum high-quality timber production. The ideal forestry stand consists of evenly spaced trees, all the same age and species. But a savanna should contain mixed woodlands with wolf trees and young replacement oaks and should be of various densities interspersed with prairie openings. To achieve this landscape, dormant-season annual fire has been our most effective restoration tool.

When Bill and I began restoration, we thought it would be enough to cut the brush and thin the overstory. We had no idea that we would also have to implement prescribed fire. We believed that fire would damage our woodland and destroy good trees. Experience has taught us, however, that only mature oaks whose heartwood has been invaded by fungi succumb to fire.

Despite our forester's early recommendation against it, we had implemented prescribed fire at Timberhill in 1995, two years after we began timber stand improvement and one year after Pauline Drobney recommended it. I've had a passion for wildflowers since my childhood when I spent many spring and summer hours in the woodland adjacent to my family's home. My sister and I gathered wildflower bouquets. We even planted a wildflower garden in the shade outside the door to our father's study. Hearing Pauline Drobney say in 1994 that fire would increase wildflower diversity in our woodlands was all the incentive I needed to burn. In February 1995, with help from our friend Bill Craig, we conducted our first burn.

Coralberry and other woody invasives were becoming reestablished in the newly opened woodland. We realized that these plants would soon take over the midstory and that the woodland would again become overstocked. At first we tried controlling the sprouts with a brush cutter. Then when they grew back, we treated them with herbicide. But the herbicide killed other plants as well and was not a satisfactory solution to controlling the woody invasives. Each year as the acreage we were restoring increased, it became obvious that fire was the only practical solution. It would control the sprouts without having to do backbreaking work or poisoning other plants.

Woody invasives becoming reestablished in the understory of a woodland that has been thinned but not burned.

The same woodland after ten annual prescribed burns

Bill and I tried to hire a contractor to do the burns, but after a year of fruitless searching, we realized that we would have to do it ourselves. In 1995 it was with a great deal of trepidation that we began using prescribed fire. With help from our friend Bill Craig, our first burn took place in the North Savanna east of the driveway. The East Savanna trail, Brush Creek, and our driveway were our firebreaks.

I had purchased a copy of *Prescribed Burning Guidelines in the Northern Great Plains*, and we followed the instructions in the section entitled "Basic Way to Conduct a Burn" (Higgens, Kruse, and Piehl 1989). (Published since then, John Weir's 2009 comprehensive book *Conducting Prescribed Fires* is an excellent step-by-step guide to implementing a prescribed burn.) Since the wind was out of the east, we lit a backfire along the driveway, our west firebreak. When the backfire inside the driveway was four feet deep, Bill walked the lighted drip torch east, dropping a line of fire along the East Savanna trail. Halfway through the savanna he turned north, following a trail downhill through the woodland. Bill Craig followed, spraying escapes from a backpack filled with water. I trailed behind, sweeping out anything that was still smoking with a wet fire broom Where the trail turned east through the savanna, little bluestem erupted in a blaze of six-foot arching flames. Downhill, at the woodland edge, this subsided into a thin ribbon of fire winding its way slowly through the dead leaves until it went out at the wet bottom field below the savanna. Smoke cloaked the trees in a mantle of gray.

Prescribed fire moving slowly through surface
litter does not damage white oak trees.

Our first burn went so well that we became overconfident. The next year was a disaster. The fire escaped into a neighbor's woodland, and we spent hours getting it under control. That was when we realized that burning wasn't for amateurs and resumed our search for expert help. For several years the Leon Volunteer Fire Department helped us. Now, a certified burn boss runs our prescribed burns. It is also possible to hire professional burn contractors.

We were amazed to see how well fire controlled the woody midstory. It killed prickly ash and eastern red cedar sprouts and scorched the ironwood stalks. At the woodland border, shingle oak leaves exploded in balls of fire. We could walk through the timber now. After three annual burns, there was little left in the midstory other than young replacement oaks. We found that even multiflora rose eventually gives in to repeated fire.

By removing the surface litter, fire allows seeds from the seed bank to make direct contact with the soil. On our late winter walks through the open woodland, the bare soil looks like it has been tilled; instead of a smooth brown surface, alternate freezing and thawing have worked the soil into a pockmarked pattern of small ridges and dimples. This action scarifies seeds in the seed bank and stimulates germination. After several annual burns, a bright green carpet of sedge covered what had been bare soil. I'll never forget Randy's reaction when he saw the sedge.

"Grass! You're not supposed to have grass in a woodland," he exclaimed.

That was the only time he was wrong. Sedge plants act like a sponge, soaking up virtually all precipitation into the soil. Instead of eroding the hillsides, the rainwater was being absorbed into the soil. Erosion was under control, and the groundwater now being held in the soil provided a constant, reliable source of water to the plants.

There is much debate about the correct timing and frequency of prescribed burns (Pyne 1982). How often and during which season should one burn a savanna for restoration? Some research into pre-settlement fire indicates that Native Americans burned woodlands every three to fifteen years. This is based on studies of burn scars in tree cross sections and analyses of soil and sedimentary charcoal (DeSantis, Hallgren, and Stahle 2010 and Clark and Royal 1994). The problem with relying on burn scars to determine historic fire regime is that the first thing European settlers did when they homesteaded was clear their land of mature trees. In Decatur County, settlers would clear ten acres at a time, sell the cleared land for a profit, and then move on to the next ten acres (Miles Leeper, personal communication 2005).

We found evidence of this when we thinned the white oak and bur oak savanna in our West 40. The previous owner had harvested several large bur oaks in that unit. I asked Dan Fogle to make a fresh cut in one of the stumps so we could count the tree rings and determine the tree's age when it was harvested in 1999. We learned that the tree was a hundred and fifty years old when it was felled. In its first twenty-five years of life, its rings bulged out on one side, indicating that side of the tree had more growth than the other side. We concluded that it must have been heavily shaded on the other side, most likely by the crown of a large tree. A scar over an injury that had occurred that same year was probably from damage during the timber harvest. After 1875 it developed evenly.

Annual fire leaves a mosaic of burned,
partially burned, and unburned patches.

The deduction that woodlands were burned every three to fifteen years conflicts with early settlers' accounts of Amerindian fires. The reason for the contradiction may be that Indian fire intervals depended on the crop: annual fire for cereal grasses, three-year intervals for basket grasses and nuts, seven-to-ten-year intervals to clear brush, and every fifteen to thirty years in large timber (Pyne 1998). That's not to say that some woodlands didn't burn every year; the anthropogenic broadcast fires often swept into timbered areas.

With few exceptions, the prevailing opinion is that a savanna restoration site should not be burned more than every two years and that the time of year should vary (National Resources Conservation Service 2009). For example, a Missouri guide to savanna restoration recommends fire every two to three years until "desired conditions are achieved" (Hartman 2005). After that, fire should be used every four to six years "to maintain vigor in the herbaceous layer and to control woody invasion." Furthermore, spring burns should be rotated with a fall burn every third or fourth burn (Hartman 2005). I have been told that the reason for the spring burn regimen is to kill smooth brome and other exotics. It kills everything else as well (Laura Rericha, personal communication 2005).

We have learned that the best results come from annual dormant-season burns. We begin burning in mid-November as soon as the oak leaves have dropped. In a good year, we can complete the woodland burns by January 1. That leaves only the West Creek unit, which is mostly prairie, to burn after snow melt. Experience has taught us that it burns best in late winter. We try to complete all our burns by March 15, but weather conditions can extend fire season to April 1.

At first we tried to follow the recommended two-to-three-year burn regimen. However, the North Savanna unit burned each year whether or not we ignited it. Dried little bluestem there provided so much fuel that we were unable to keep it from igniting annually. After several burns, I noted that this site was much more diverse than those we burned periodically. The monoculture of little bluestem had been transformed with abundant populations of highly conservative wildflowers such as yellow pimpernel. Since then we have ignited all of our burn units annually. By the time we purchased West Creek, we had learned to burn three years in a row before beginning timber stand improvement. This controls many of the woody invasives and makes the mechanical work easier and less intensive.

Practical experience at Timberhill has found two assumptions regarding annual prescribed fire to be incorrect. These assumptions, based on inductive reasoning, are that we are perverting oak reproduction and doing irrevocable damage to the overwintering invertebrate population.

We do not protect oak sprouts from fire. Some such as this young white oak will always survive annual fire and replace dying mature oaks.

That we are perverting oak reproduction because fire kills oak sprouts, would be true if we were managing for an ideal forestry stand of even-aged, evenly spaced trees. However, each of our woodland units contains various species of young replacement oaks. Some oak sprouts always survive annual fire and grow into replacement trees. Those that survive are stouter and grow more quickly. And their random placement replicates the pre-settlement savannas whose boundaries varied depending on the precipitation and the extent of aboriginal fires. Fire also results in a habitat that continues to evolve-young oak trees are replacing the dominant hickory in the West 40 grove, the bur and white oaks becoming established in several prairie openings will eventually transform them into open savanna, and as mature woodland trees die, they are creating new prairie openings.

Survival of an abundant invertebrate population on land that is subject to prescribed fire is a legitimate contemporary concern. We have learned, however, that annual dormant-season fire restores the habitat while doing the least damage. Flames of annual fire move through the dried plant material above ground, leaving thousands of culms and stems per acre for invertebrate habitat. Periodic fire incinerates, parboils, and kills because of the heavy fuel buildup between burns. It doesn't leave the complex structural mosaic of totally burned, partially burned, and unburned sections that result from annual prescribed burns. Every year is different. Humidity, wind speed and direction, available fuel, and topography all influence fire intensity. What doesn't burn this year will burn next year.

Ground layer after an annual burn showing intact invertebrate habitat

Because of our fire regimen, Timberhill has flowering plants in the wooded areas from early spring through fall frost. These are what the butterflies and other insects depend on. From early spring throughout the growing season, Timberhill supports abundant populations of butterflies, including overwintering species such as spring azure and mourning cloak. Particularly abundant are meadow and great spangled fritillaries, both breeding residents. We have even observed the rare regal fritillary despite the fact that Timberhill has no prairie violets, its preferred larval food source. A 2005 survey of ants found fifty-two species at Timberhill. (At that time the Iowa list included a hundred species.) Two of the species that biologist Laura Rericha found had not been previously recorded in Iowa. (Wilhelm and Rericha 2007). In 2011 a preliminary survey of native bees by Laura identified twenty-nine species, some of which were very conservative. Several uncommon beetles have been collected here as well (Edwin Freese, personal communication 2011).

Local residents who hunted here before we purchased the property have told me that Timberhill supports more wildlife since we have restored it. Particularly abundant are wild turkeys. In early spring we often see gobblers displaying for a circle of females. During deer season Bill Craig complained that so many roosted in the trees near his deer stand that they interfered with his hunting. They gobbled at his every movement and chased the deer away.

Burning in fall and winter also prevents damage to the spring ephemerals that begin to bloom in late March. Burning after April 1 would result in high mortality to the rare wild hyacinth and false hellebore, whose vascular tissue is highly vulnerable at that time of year. And what about the woodcocks that nest here in late March?

We have adopted a fire regimen that best meets our goals of restoring a diverse habitat while doing the least damage. After fifteen years of dormant-season burns, Timberhill has over 460 vascular plants, provides high-quality habitat for fifty-two species neotropical migrant birds, and is home to countless redheaded woodpeckers, and hundreds of ectomycorrhizal fungi. Instead of perverting diversity, annual fire is restoring it.

This diversity is the result of fire and timber stand improvement combined. Although fire alone will eventually restore the savanna structure, it will not thin the fire-resistant oak trees. In an overstocked savanna, the ambient light needed to support a diverse understory and support oak regeneration can be achieved only with fire and timber stand improvement. The assessment of Timberhill management compared the light energy that reached the ground in four plots that had been thinned and burned for ten years with two plots that had had no management and two that had been thinned but not burned. The thinned and burned plots averaged 14.3 percent full sunlight, the unmanaged plots 1.8 percent, and the thinned only plots 2.3 percent (Wilhelm and Rericha 2007). Neither the unmanaged nor the thinned-only plots had enough sunlight to support either oak regeneration or a diverse understory.

6.

THE LAND HAS A LONG MEMORY

TIMBERHILL NEEDED ONLY FIRE AND THINNING to restore the savanna habitat. Neither herbicide treatment of exotics and ruderales (plants growing on waste ground) nor seeding of savanna species was necessary. In the early years of our restoration, we pulled weeds such as sweet clover and treated shingle oak sprouts and multiflora rose with herbicide. These practices were unnecessary; each year fire top-killed the shingle oak sprouts, made the multiflora rose more susceptible to fungal infection, and stimulated natural processes that eventually controlled weeds. The undesirable plants gave up as deeper-rooted conservative plants became reestablished in the understory. The time required depends on the land-use history of the site. Some sites recover within three years; others take ten or more years. Even heavily grazed woodlands can recover. It just takes time and patience. The land needs to go through a healing process. Just as an injured person needs to let wounds heal, so must one be patient with the land and give it whatever time it needs to recuperate.

Like the foundation of a house, healthy woodland soil is necessary to support a diverse population of understory plants. The first step in building this foundation was to restore the graminoids (grasses and sedges), particularly the sedges. With each prescribed fire, we found that sedges became more abundant until they dominated the understory. Soil held in the sedge root mass acts like a sponge to absorb and retain nearly all precipitation. This controls surface runoff and stores groundwater in the soil. Working in concert, soil fungi, microbes, and insects decompose dead organic matter and build up soil aggregates. This nutrient-rich porous soil then becomes a solid foundation for wild orchids and other conservative plants.

When we purchased Timberhill, the ravines that separated the sharply dissected ridges were head-cutting deeper into the hill with each rain event. Progressive erosion carried away topsoil and wildflower seeds. In as little as three years after we began restoration, however, the surface runoff was being controlled, and the woodland floor transformed from bare dirt with an occasional wildflower to a carpet of green. As native perennial vegetation became established in the ravines, it absorbed nearly all precipitation and arrested head-cut erosion.

Head-cut erosion has stopped at the
Timberhill fenceline, indicated by the red arrow.

Restoration has also restored seeps, the small springs where groundwater exits the soil. Seeps are formed by precipitation that percolates through topsoil, moving slowly downward until it hits the clay-rock glacial layer underneath. From there it moves laterally through the subsurface and discharges along hillsides and the base of low slopes. In the South Meadow, which had been intensively farmed and grazed, there were no seeps at the time of purchase. Now that sedges and grasses are well established there, water percolates slowly through the soil in numerous places along the trail that dissects this prairie restoration.

This healing process has taken ten years or longer in the most degraded sites such as the South Meadow and three years or less in more virgin sites such as the West Creek unit. There, seeps with active flows have survived despite heavy grazing. These included a spring that once supplied water to the pioneer settlers. It was still actively releasing water from the soil when we purchased West Creek. The previous owner told me that water flowed to the spring through silica sand veins that he called sand lenses. However, eastern red cedar that covered the hillside above the spring had decreased the water flow to the spring. Knowing that the cedars' thirst for water decreased active flow to the sand lenses, we asked Dan Fogle to cut down the cedars. The following August, after the cedar foliage had dried, we burned the trees. (At that time of year, green plants on the hillside kept the fire from spreading.) It took only three annual burns for Indian grass and sedges to cover the hillside again. Not only have groundwater flows to the spring increased, but discharge is seeping like a sieve out of the soil around the spring.

The difference between the time it took to restore the East Savanna and the West 40 savanna remnant is a good example of varied recovery times. The dry sandy ridge that tops the East Savanna above Brush Creek is where Bill and I began the Timberhill savanna restoration. Originally we thought we might build our house there. Until the previous owner told us that it was prone to lightning strikes, that is. It's a good thing we took his advice. Not only have four large oak trees been killed by lightning strikes since we bought the property, but this site has also proven to have the highest floristic quality.

When we began restoration in 1993, I was overwhelmed by the enormity of our undertaking. To me, the only choice was to begin with the land closest to the house and work outward from there. At the time we didn't know that the East Savanna was the best place to begin our restoration. Although it had a history of heavy grazing and extensive timber harvest, the spare herbaceous layer contained remnant native plants, and there were no exotics other than redtop and Kentucky bluegrass. Beginning there enabled us to see the land's potential.

The midstory of ironwood, shingle oak, and eastern red cedar blocked most of the sunlight from the understory. We began restoration on this ridgetop by clearing the brush, which we stacked in a huge pile and burned. (We no longer stack and burn brush; we have learned that this sterilizes the soil.) This left a canopy of widely scattered white oaks, the wolf trees we wanted to keep. Remnant wildflower populations were clustered in the sunniest spots and not distributed evenly on the ridgetop. Each gap was dominated by a different species: wild indigo under the canopy gap at the east end, yellow pimpernel at the north end, and scaly blazing star in between. There were even a few purple milkweeds along the trail across the ridge. Patches of bare earth remained where we had cleared dense brush. Annual prescribed burns, once we began them, maintained brush control and stimulated the plants. From the first there was enough little bluestem to fuel fire through the site, leaving patches of burned, partially burned, and unburned land.

It took only three years for the land to reveal its potential. A few conservative forbs pioneered the restoration, increasing their abundance and cover after every burn: wild indigo moved from the east end gap west to the driveway between the savanna and the house, scaly blazing star spread in all directions, even south into the darker hillside woodland, and bastard toadflax became so thick we couldn't help but step on it. I was particularly pleased to see a dense stand of New Jersey tea become established halfway down the hillside south of the ridgetop. Sunlight and fire had worked their magic; ecological succession was going in the right direction in the East Savanna.

We first burned the remnant white oak and bur oak savanna in the West 40 unit in 2001. We thinned it in 2002. From conversations with the previous owner we learned that the understory had once been exceedingly species-rich. As a child it was his job to herd sheep there. He told me the first wildflowers to bloom each year were trout lilies. He also remembered seeing bluebells, sweet William, Dutchman's breeches and a deep orange wildflower, most likely Michigan lily or butterfly milkweed. "I used to bring my mother a bouquet of those home every night," he told me.

After our experience with the East Savanna, we expected it would take only three years to restore an understory full of colorful blooms after we began annual burns and completed timber stand improvement. That has not been the case. Ten years since the first annual prescribed burn, the sedges are just becoming more evident. Other than one purple milkweed and a few Culver's root, there is little bloom. Dogbane, an aggressive native, has taken over the sunniest spots. But we know that higher floristic quality will eventually prevail. And it is so much more interesting to watch the process evolve, to thrill to the discovery of new plants, as the natural processes are restored.

We have done no seeding at Timberhill except to spread Indian grass, little bluestem, and big bluestem seed in the former crop fields. (We harvest the seed from our prairie remnants.) Yet the Timberhill plant list has increased from the initial survey of 100 in 1994 to over 460 vascular plants in 2011. Seeding of native forbs is an option in a restoration but may have unintended consequences.

In Stage 1 of restoration woodland sunflower often dominates the understory.

At Timberhill, woodland sunflower and tick trefoil were the first wildflowers to become reestablished in the open woodlands. It may take years before deeper-rooted, more conservative species become established. Choosing to speed up the process by using herbicide on the woodland sunflower and seeding plants from savanna indicator species lists was not necessary and would have interfered with the natural processes. Even plants from locally collected seed can become invasive if the soil isn't ready. Until the underground network of fungi and other microbes are well established, there are no natural controls; highly aggressive species such as Indian plantain may take over a site, suppressing other wildflowers.

Sedge replacing tick trefoil (plant with pink inflorescences) in Stage 2

We found that with annual fire and 10 percent ambient light, a diverse understory eventually replaces the woodland sunflower. We continue to observe this process unfold at Timberhill. It takes place in three stages. In stage 1, woodland sunflower and tick trefoil dominates the understory. After a few burns, sedges became more abundant. In stage 2, the woodland sunflower and tick trefoil decreases as they are replaced by sedge, bottlebrush grass, and moss.

Large twayblade orchid

It is at this stage that the first orchids, large twayblades and frog orchids, show up. Neither is a very conservative species, but their presence indicates that the soil hydrology has been restored. (No matter how rare, all orchids need a dependable supply of groundwater.) In stage 3, conservative forbs become established, and the woodland sunflower and tick trefoil disappear completely. Patches of ground at different stages of restoration are found throughout the understory once the soil has healed. The perimeter of each patch then expands in the woodland until they meld into a single species-rich understory.

Stage 3: Conservative plants such as blazing star and sky-blue asters replace woodland sunflower as they become established in the open woodland.

At Timberhill certain plants indicate to us that the land is healing: sedge and bottlebrush grass herald initiation of the healing process, and wood betony and bastard toadflax signify that the process is well underway. In the final stage wood betony gives way to a species-rich stand of wildflowers, grasses, and sedges; bastard toadflax will continue to spread throughout the site. We have even seen warm-season grasses such as big bluestem become established under the oak canopy.

Bottlebrush grass indicates that the land is healing

I was tempted to use herbicide to eradicate the monotony of tick trefoil or woodland sunflower and seed the site with plants from savanna indicator lists. But one can only guess which plants belong where. Each variety, particularly the most conservative ones, occupies its own niche in the system. It will thrive only where conditions suit it best. Of the three pink-flowered false foxgloves found at Timberhill, for example, each requires a completely different habitat.

Eared false foxglove prefers a wet habitat

Eared false foxglove grows in the wet, spring-fed West Creek prairie. Slender false foxglove is more of a generalist, growing in both virgin and disturbed grasslands. Round-stemmed false foxglove, the most conservative, tolerates more shade and grows only on the dry oak-studded ridgetops.

Slender false foxglove grows in both virgin and disturbed grasslands

Round-stemmed false foxglove habitat is limited to dry oak-studded ridgetops

I'm thankful we waited for germination from the seed bank and the release of suppressed plants rather than succumbing to species list mentality. It resulted in a more diverse understory with each species finding its own place in the landscape. Human intervention cannot improve on how and where nature arranges plants. Gerould Wilhelm demonstrated this to me by taking square-meter transects in the East Savanna and listing all the plants in each. No two square meters had more than 50 percent of the same species. Each transect was unique with its own assemblage of plants. As restoration proceeded and the composition of wildflowers rearranged itself each year, Bill and I could not help but marvel at the resilience and complexity of this ecosystem.

7.

BIRDS AT TIMBERHILL

FROM THE TURKEY VULTURES SOARING THE thermal updrafts overhead to the constant drumming of redheaded woodpeckers and the colorful neotropical migrant songbirds, our oak savanna is a haven to both woodland and open-country birds. Species as varied as the redheaded woodpecker, wild turkey, and dickcissel use this habitat for nesting and brood rearing. Savanna restoration creates a mosaic of habitats for a heterogeneity of bird species: raptors, neotropical migrants, and permanent residents all thrive in this habitat. The decline of high-quality savannas has resulted in a significant decline of species associated with this ecosystem.

A study of the effects of prescribed fire and savanna restoration on the population and community ecology of Illinois birds includes a list of forty species with "important or exclusive habitat association" with oak savannas or open woodlands during breeding season (Brawn 1998, 3–5). The population status of each species, whether decreasing, stable, or increasing, was also noted using data compiled between 1966 and 1996 by the Audubon Breeding Bird Survey. Over half of the species listed declined significantly; of particular concern are the redheaded woodpecker, summer tanager, and northern bobwhite that were found to nest only in restored sites (Brawn 1998). Fourteen of the declining species on Brawn's list, including the most seriously threatened, breed at Timberhill.

The extent of the Timberhill woodlands is limited by the sharply dissected landscape, but it is still able to support a large bird population. Management has connected the woodlands with different exposures, reliefs, and increased floristic diversity. Before restoration, a dense hedge that separated woodland from prairie created a barrier between the two. Repeated fires have eliminated the hedge, decreasing the effects of this fragmentation. To the birds, Timberhill woodland and prairie have become one unbroken habitat. Even birds sensitive to forest fragmentation such as the wood thrush and yellow-throated vireo make this their summer home.

According to Gerould Wilhelm, "opening the timbered tracts, paradoxically, created a great tract of timber without distinct edges. The intervening prairie noses and ambient dissections blended into the whole. The overall effect was to link ravines, bluffs and nose slopes to create a more continuous tract of timbered habitat," at least as perceived by the birds (Wilhelm and Rericha 2007, 40).

At Timberhill, avian habitats include savanna and open woodland, transition zones where grassland merges gradually into savanna, and prairie grasslands. In the woodlands, fire has a created structural complexity that includes scattered mature trees, standing dead trees, and snags as well as unburned erect plant stalks. Girdled and large dead trees break up very gradually, providing numerous microsites used by cavity nesters for many years after the trees die. They may be blackened by fire, yet they persist in standing through many prescribed burns. The branches fall off, but each thick trunk stands until fire is able to penetrate the interior and a chimney fire hollows out the trunk.

The study conducted by Gerould Wilhelm and Laura Rericha at Timberhill in 2006 found the breeding bird population to be strikingly different between the managed woodlands and adjacent unmanaged land. Thirty species of birds were found to be breeding in the thinned and annually burned plots, whereas only four species, all cavity nesters, were noted breeding in the unmanaged plots. Of the seventy-three bird species recorded in the study, 51 percent nested in managed woodland; only 11 percent, all cavity nesters, nested in unmanaged plots (Wilhelm and Rericha 2007). (See the appendix for a list of Timberhill birds.)

Rose-breasted grosbeaks, for example, are one of the most common sightings at Timberhill. When Brawn, author of the Illinois study, compared rose-breasted grosbeak nest success in burned and unmanaged savannas, he found that only 9 percent produced offspring in closed-canopy forests. In managed savanna and woodland there was 41 percent success. For indigo buntings the difference was also significant: 7 percent success in closed-canopy forests and 30 percent success in managed savannas and woodlands (Brawn 1998).

Habitat for ground-nesting species is found in unburned patches of dead leaves and grasses. Although we seldom see a whippoorwill, we hear its distinctive song nightly after dusk and during the hour before dawn. It lays its eggs on the ground in the open woodland and then covers them with dead leaves. The American woodcock, another ground-nesting species, prefers the successional habitat in the West 40. Young trees interspersed with several prairie openings provide woodland nesting sites near nighttime foraging sites. In early spring one can usually hear a male woodcock's occasional chirps and observe aerial mating displays in a ravine below the hickory grove.

South Meadow showing structure left after prescribed burn

The woodland borders and prairie scrub provide habitat for species that nest or forage in shrubs and small trees, such as indigo buntings, brown thrashers, and summer tanagers (Brawn 1998). During breeding season we spot indigo bunting nests in blackberry thickets and shingle oak grubs. Annual fire may remove the previous year's growth, but the plants re-sprout from perennial roots each year. After a prescribed burn in the South Meadow, for example, we can see the numerous shrubs that will re-sprout or leaf out in the spring. Ten-to-twelve-foot flames may have burned through the meadow, yet hundreds of woody stalks are evidence of habitat for these birds.

Species nesting there in 2012 included gray catbird, field sparrow, Eastern towhee, indigo bunting, and dickcissel. That summer I observed three male Eastern towhees singing persistently from the large crowned white oaks surrounding the border, a male and female indigo bunting calling to each other, and summer tanagers flying into the meadow to forage for wasps. Occasionally female hummingbirds flew swiftly from one showy goldenrod to another, gleaning insects from the spider webs on the corollas.

Filbert leafing out in spring after prescribed burn

Burning and thinning of the West Creek unit created tallgrass prairie habitat with brush and a few tall trees. There restoration has had a significant effect on the bird population. In June 2012 I walked through this tract with biologist Laura Rericha. As we followed a path between the bottom cornfield and the prairie, she stopped and listened. Simple "tsi-lick" bird calls, somewhat resembling a cricket's chirp, emanated from several locations in the field, indicating a small loose colony of Henslow's sparrows. There were at least three breeding pairs. Laura explained that the field now had the perfect structure for Henslow's sparrows: a combination of grasses, forbs, and scattered shrubs. This species nests at the base of a clump of grass with grass partly arched over the nest. Intense cultivation throughout their range has reduced breeding habitat, and they are becoming quite rare in much of their former range. In 2012 Bill also sighted a nesting pair of blue grosbeaks in a thicket between an old cornfield and the wetland.

As the Timberhill woodlands opened up and sunlight became a constant presence, the understory wildflowers gradually became reestablished until something was blooming from early spring until hard frost in late fall. This increased density provides neotropical migrant birds with plentiful food for breeding and brood rearing. The diverse insect population on flowers, seeds, and leaf material supports a much higher breeding density than unmanaged woodlands. Even after the canopy has fully leafed out, plants such as false foxgloves, blazing stars, and asters bloom in the open woodland. All the foods preferred by the various species are found in the restored habitat: night-flying insects—particularly large moths—for whippoorwills, multiple bees and wasps for summer tanagers, insects and earthworms in the rich humus for woodcocks, and serviceberry, blackberry, and elderberry fruit for Baltimore and orchard orioles. All are abundant on the native plants and in the soil.

Songbirds such as rose-breasted grosbeaks and summer tanagers that winter in Central and South America breed and raise their young in Midwest deciduous woodlands. In late spring they return to their birthplace to breed. Their survival depends not only on saving the rainforests but on restoring open deciduous woodlands with a constant dependable food source. If a pair breeds successfully, it will return, as will its offspring. At the woodland border, we often hear the distinctive pick-tuck call of the summer tanager. In 1996 we first observed a breeding pair of summer tanagers in the East Savanna. As more of the woodland opened up, the population increased significantly; we now observe five breeding pairs each season.

We never tire of hearing bluebirds sing from the roof of the house or the uppermost branches of the oak trees surrounding the South Meadow. Year-round residents, they prefer habitat with open-country patchy vegetation and large trees. Even in winter we hear their low-pitched warbling song. During the breeding season, they nest in bluebird boxes scattered throughout the property, producing two or three broods each season; in winter they feed on berries of a few mature red cedars left in the woodlands after timber stand improvement as well as poison ivy and sumac berries, and they take shelter in white oak cavities. However, come a January warm spell, they're back at the nest boxes or warbling from the roof of the house.

Red-headed woodpecker

Redheaded woodpeckers are considered a species of high conservation concern because of population decline throughout their range (Brawn 1998). A habitat specialist, this species is seriously threatened by the loss of open deciduous woodlands. It has declined 4.6 percent each year since 1980 (Audubon Watch List). Redheads are habitat specialists. They will only nest and breed successfully in woodlands with snags, large standing dead trees, and open areas for fly catching and ground foraging.

At Timberhill, redheads are year-round residents. Regarded as a keystone species, they have a disproportionate effect on the environment relative to their biomass. By excavating a new nest in a dead tree or snag each year, they play a critical role in maintaining the structure of the ecological community. Not only does a restored savanna contain plentiful standing dead trees and snags, but it meets all of this species' food needs. Insects are abundant during the growing season, and timber stand improvement has increased acorn production. Redheaded woodpeckers cache acorns for winter food in holes and crevices of oak trees. We observe them each fall flying across the South Meadow transporting acorns to their winter stash between the East Savanna and West Woodland. In summer the many immature specimens indicate that they are breeding successfully.

Pileated woodpecker excavation in dead white oak

In 2005 Bill and I were taking our daily walk in the East Savanna when we saw a pair of large black birds flying through the riparian woodland along Brush Creek. I thought at first that they were crows, but the flash of white on the underside of the wings indicated a different species. This was our first sighting of the large, boldly marked pileated woodpecker, another keystone habitat modifier. Now we frequently observe them as they fly across the South Meadow and hear their loud ringing call scold us if we venture too close to a nest. They excavate large rectangular nest cavities in standing dead trees. These become sites for secondary cavity nesters such as squirrels and owls the next year. Pileateds' preferred foods are carpenter ants and wood-boring beetle larvae. In their foraging for these insects, pileateds penetrate into the sapwood and heartwood of dead trees. This makes wood-dwelling insects in the substrate available to other species. A dead tree with large fresh wood chips around its base is a sure sign of pileateds.

When we first moved to Decatur County, one of our neighbors told us that he had seen a bald eagle nest along the Weldon River south of Timberhill. Bill and I were both surprised to learn that these raptors wintered nearby. Now watching bald eagles has become a favorite winter pastime. In order to control the overpopulation of deer, Bill Craig and Jim Petty harvest as many does as possible during the January antlerless season. After butchering, they return the carcasses to Timberhill to be recycled as bald eagle food. They dump the remains at the edge of the hickory grove west of the house. Within a day, bald eagles appear, and Bill and I can watch from the kitchen table as they feed on the carcasses.

Birds contribute to creating a balanced environment and controlling insects. As do the bats (which are mammals, not birds) that nest under the loose bark of shagbark hickory trees by taking flight at dusk, circling over the pond and around the buildings, eating mosquitoes. We call them our mosquito patrol. During daytime hours, barn swallows and northern rough-winged swallows patrol the pond, skimming the water as they feed on a variety of insects above the water.

Understanding and providing for the needs of the open-country and savanna-dependent bird species greatly enhances the quality of a restoration. Besides being a delight to observe, birds play a crucial role in dispersing seeds and keeping the insect population in balance. Active management at Timberhill has increased nest microsite diversity, increased plant flowering and seed production, and restored rich humus soil. Savanna restoration has stimulated a species-rich avifauna with many of the open-country and savanna species one would expect to find in this habitat.

8.

FUNGI AT TIMBERHILL

OFTEN OVERLOOKED, MUSHROOMS ARE AN ESSENTIAL component of the savanna ecosystem. In a woodland, it is the fungi that connect all the elements into the larger whole. Mycelium, the threadlike vegetative structure of fungi, forms a network that links plants together and regulates the flow of nutrients and water throughout the root layer of the soil. Besides its direct benefit to plant nutrition, the fungal network controls erosion by aggregating soil particles. A well-aggregated soil has higher rates of water infiltration, soil stability, and fertility, thus increasing the quality of the habitat for native plants (Dighton 2003). Glomalin, a sticky substance produced by arbuscular mycorrhizal fungi (soil fungi that have a symbiotic relationship with plants) binds the soil aggregates together (Chaudhary and Griswold 2001). The more diverse the fungal network, the more plants a habitat can support (Stamets 2005).

Studying the fungi that fruit in a restoration increases one's understanding of the land's healing process. It may be difficult to identify a specimen to the species level, but one can easily learn the genera commonly found in a geographic area. Mushroom clubs throughout the continental United States provide the amateur with the skills to learn mushroom identification; for a listing of mushroom clubs and other information on field trips and classes, visit the North American Mycological Association website.

The two most important groups of woodland fungi are the decomposers—the saprobic fungi that break down the debris of dead vegetable matter, and the mycorrhizas that form a symbiotic relationship with plants. These types work together in a complex relationship that builds healthy woodland soils and provides plant nutrition. The two groups are so interconnected that it is often difficult to determine where one ends and another begins.

Decomposer mushrooms form a network through soil, leaf litter, and decaying wood. The mycelium weaves in and out of plant-debris cell walls, breaking down cellulose and lignin into simple compounds of carbon, hydrogen, and minerals that plants can use. Each saprobic species secretes different acids and enzymes into the dead organic matter to break down the nutrients into simple inorganic compounds. Nutrients and minerals not used by the fungi leach into the soil, where they become available to plants and insects. Without recycling by the saprobic fungi, these nutrients and minerals would be locked out of the system.

Bricktop outcompetes honey mushroom, a virulent tree pathogen

Some of the decomposers protect the woodland from the disease rot fungi. Turkey tail and bricktop, for example, outcompete honey mushroom, a virulent tree pathogen (Stamets 2005). This parasite first attacks tree roots, then spreads through the wood, causing progressive white rot. Honey mushrooms used to be a common occurrence at Timberhill, fruiting in large clusters around the bases of tree stumps and on buried wood. I seldom see them any longer; bricktop and turkey tail are so numerous that they keep honey mushrooms in check.

Oyster mushrooms fruiting on downed shagbark hickory

There are three types of saprobic fungi, all of which can coexist in the same location. The fast-growing primary decomposers such as oyster mushrooms begin the decomposition process by breaking down cellulose sugar (Stamets 2005). These are followed by the secondary decomposers that work with bacteria, yeasts, and other fungi to break down cellulose and lignin. Several different species may be present on the same dead plant material. It is not unusual to see turkey tail, reishi, and a crust-like toothed polypore decomposing the same log. The tertiary decomposers such as meadow mushrooms work in habitats already broken down.

Several different species—turkey tail, reishi, and a small pink slime mold—are working on this log.

Rather than leave downed wood where it falls, most landowners cut and stack it into neat structures or remove it entirely. Instead, the wood should be left on the ground for decomposer fungi to do their work enriching the soil. Deadwood also contributes to habitat diversity. In a woodland, ants, many beetles, and other insects associated with deadwood can increase animal diversity by 30 percent (Dudley, Equilibrium, and Vallaurt 2004).

When documenting an oak savanna restoration, most people list only the plants and animals they have observed. But in any restoration, what is happening in the root or rhizome layer plays a key role in determining the quality of the site. The interactions between fungi, plant roots, animals, and soil microbes substantially influence ecosystem process. Mycorrhizal fungi form a symbiotic relationship with the roots of living plants and thus play the most active role in nutrient cycling. Over 90 percent of native plants have mycorrhizal associates. The more diverse the mycorrhizal fungi, the more plants a habitat can support (Van der Heijden et al. 1998). These fungi, not the roots, supply plants with the most nutrients (Smith and Read 2009). Since each species delivers different benefits to its symbiotic host, a biodiversity of fungi is very important to plant nutrition (Tedersoo et al. 2006). This is all the more reason for low-impact annual fire, which doesn't damage the mycorrhizal fungi by raising the soil temperature.

There are various types of mycorrhizal fungi classified according to the method of root attachment. Ectomycorrhizal (ECM) fungi sheath the roots of oak trees. These are the woodland fungi that produce mushroom-fruiting bodies. The vegetative portions of ECM fungi extend outward from the plant roots, absorbing water and nutrients that pass through the fungus-plant interface. Their many functions in the oak savanna include capturing and supplying vital nutrients—particularly nitrogen and phosphorus—to their host plant, protecting the host against pathogens and toxic substances, and acting as a buffer against moisture stress. Essential nutrients provided by the fungi also reduce the host plant's competition for resources and influence plant composition. In this symbiotic association, the fungus receives sugars from the tree (Dighton 2003).

As with the saprobic fungi, each species exudes a unique mix of enzymes and acids that converts different organic matter into simple compounds that plants can use. Several species are usually associated with the same tree, even the same root tip. "It is thought that a high ectomycorrhizal diversity is important in the healthy functioning of a woodland. Different fungi appear to have different roles. Some may be better at helping the tree take up particular nutrients, others may be specialized at protecting against pathogens, others in enzyme production" (Jonsson 1998, 14).

Little is known about what conditions contribute to high ectomycorrhizal diversity in a woodland (Van der Heijden 2002). Preference for soil conditions and host plants likely plays a role (Tedersoo et al. 2006). We know that ECM fungi are dependent on carbohydrate production of their tree associate; therefore the levels of tree growth and photosynthesis may be important—the tree must produce excess carbohydrates in order for the fungi to thrive. Since timber stand improvement has increased oak crown expansion, it follows that Timberhill oak trees have higher carbohydrate production. It has also been noted that mycorrhizas develop best in sites with over 25 percent full daylight (Ramsbottom 1953), which is also true of portions of Timberhill savanna, especially the east woodland ridgetops. Here I have even collected ectomycorrhizal fungi such as indigo milky cap and *Leccinum* fruiting from the base of little bluestem.

Plant composition may also influence fungal diversity since the number of ectomycorrhizal species in a site is directly proportional to the amount of dead organic matter in the soil. The decomposable products of dead root cells of the various species differ; the type of substance exuded by a particular root determines which species' enzymes are able to break down the substance (Ramsbottom 1953). As the inorganic and organic resources in the soil become more diverse, so does the composition of fungi (Dighton 2003).

Fire accelerates the return of nutrients to the soil and provides more nutrients to the fungi. More nutrients require more diverse fungi to break down the plentiful organic matter. It follows that this results in a more diverse mycorrhizal population. Groundwater resources are also important to mushroom diversity; the larger root mass of fire-stimulated grasses and sedges is able to capture more precipitation, providing a consistent groundwater supply throughout the growing season. These plants sustain soil moisture during periods of summer drought because "night air can condense on the bunch sedges and grasses and small but steady inflows of moisture to the system can buffer the effects of extended periods without rain" (Wilhelm and Rericha 2007, 41).

Fungi that fruit in a particular open woodland vary greatly according to the species of trees in that woodland. Most ECM fungi at Timberhill are associated with white oak. Timber stand improvement has eliminated some tree species such as ironwood, therefore eliminating their ectomycorrhizal associates. However, oak savanna management has increased the abundance of highly conservative (strong fidelity to habitat) mushroom species.

Depending on the weather, fruiting of ECM fungi in south central Iowa begins in late May or early June. The season usually ends after a hard fall frost, although it may extend into late November. I have collected fungi fruiting from the ground as late as December 6. The heaviest fruiting occurs in late summer, after the midsummer dry spell. Just as do the wildflowers, different mushroom species fruit at different times of the season.

Mushrooms in the groups of brittle caps, milky caps, and death caps are the earliest to fruit each year. If there is adequate precipitation, various species in these groups will continue to fruit throughout the growing season. Late summer and early fall are the most productive seasons for ECM fungi. Boletes, fungi with a spongy surface of pores instead of gills on the underside of the cap, are most abundant at this time of year. Many genera are included in this large group of ectomycorrhizal fungi; so far I have collected species from seven genera. Other groups fruiting in late summer and fall include the waxy caps and webcaps (*Cortinarius*).

As restoration of our open oak woodlands proceeded, I observed an increasing diversity of fungi. ECM fungi continue to fruit into late fall, after a hard frost, when I have collected ten different species of waxy cap mushrooms. In 2000 I began finding species never before recorded in Iowa. Even species usually limited to coniferous or mixed coniferous-deciduous woodlands now fruit regularly at Timberhill. The first such collection was what looked like an aborted bolete. I knew that it must be a bolete because it was fleshy and had pores, but it didn't have a normal stalk and cap. Partially buried in the soil, it was irregularly shaped, with a twisted and contorted pore surface and a stalk that extended only a short distance below the tubes. This species turned out to be *Gastroboletus turbinatus*, a species thought to be found only in evergreen woodlands.

Boletus dupainii, a very rare bolete, fruits regularly at Timberhill

I also began to find species not described in any of the mushroom guides. One such was a bolete first collected in 2000. The sticky red cap with orange pores and flesh that instantly turned a bright blue when bruised distinguished it from any species described in the bolete references. It was several years before I was able to identify it as *Boletus dupainii*, a European species found only one other time in the continental United States, in North Carolina. It has not been found there since but continues to fruit more abundantly each year at Timberhill. This may be the only site in the continental United States where this species fruits regularly (Ernst Both, personal communication 2009). In 2010 I collected another red-pored bolete, *Boletus rhodosanguineus*, fruiting in a cluster of little bluestem in the East Savanna. Previously this species had been recorded only in Ohio and western New York. I have also found an unnamed bolete species fruiting in a cluster of shagbark hickories. Of the twenty-five boletes collected at Timberhill, six have not been previously recorded in Iowa: *Boletus dupainii*, *Boletus erythropus*, *Boletus griseus*, *Boletus rhodosanguineus*, *Gastroboletus turbinatus*, and *Leccinum sp. #3*. (See a list of Timberhill boletes in the appendix.)

Boletus rhodosanguineus fruiting at Timberhill

Wherever I found new mushroom species, I observed an increased diversity of wildflowers with a strong fidelity to habitat. The more I learned, the more questions I had. Was there a connection between mushroom species richness and the diversity of other savanna organisms? Was mushroom species abundance an indicator of ecosystem quality? Which ectomycorrhizal species were indicators of a high-quality site?

The Wilhelm and Rericha assessment of Timberhill management included tree demography, light availability, vegetation, bird observation, and ant sampling in all the plots. I thought documenting the ECM fungi in each plot might provide some answers to my questions. In 2006 I visited each plot weekly from late May through the late fall mushroom season. I documented all the aboveground ectomycorrhizal fungi fruiting in each plot. (Since this survey collected data only for one year, it could not include all the species growing in each plot. Mushroom fruiting is ephemeral, dependent on many factors, and many species don't fruit each year.)

To compute the floristic quality of the fungi, I had to assign coefficients of conservatism (COC) to each species. A coefficient of conservatism assigns a number that measures each species' fidelity to a specific habitat. The higher the number, the higher a plant's COC. Working with Lois Tiffany, Rosanne Healy, and Iowa State University herbarium records, we assigned COCs to each ectomycorrhizal species on the Timberhill mushroom list. We assigned a number between 4 and 6 if we were unsure about the quality of an area where the species had been collected but certain that it was some kind of remnant, 7 or 8 for fungi usually found in a pretty nice woodland, and 9 or 10 to fungi found only in a totally awesome woodland. (See Swink and Wilhelm 1994 for an explanation of COC and how to compute a floristic quality index.) Because of their relationship to the habitat, none of the ectomycorrhizal fungi scored a COC lower than 5. For example, chanterelles (COC = 5) are found in degraded woodlands but require four organisms to fruit: the host tree, pseudomonas bacteria, red soil yeast, and the fungus itself (Stamets 2005).

Using the COCs we had assigned each species, I was able to compute the floristic quality of the fungi in each plot and compare it to the floristic quality of the wildflower population. I didn't know whether the number we'd assigned each mushroom species was accurate, but I was pleasantly surprised to find that the fungi with the highest coefficients of conservatism were found only in plots with the highest floristic quality. The results of the survey confirmed to me that there is a relationship between the fungi and the floristic quality of the plants: the higher the floristic quality of the woodland, the more diverse the fungal community,

I also learned that bolete species are the strongest indicators of high-quality habitat at Timberhill. Before we began restoring Timberhill in 1993, the only bolete mushroom species I found on the property was the bitter bolete, one of the least conservative species. Since then I have observed a succession of boletes from the early successional, less conservative species to the highly conservative, late successional species. Late successional species fruit only in sites with the most conservative wildflowers, such as round-stemmed false foxglove.

A good example of mushroom succession is the woodland in the southeast corner of our property. Timber stand improvement was completed there in 2000, and the first burn was in 2001. We have burned it every year since. In October after the first burn, the woodland floor was covered with a heavy fruiting of the deadly destroying angel mushrooms. After three burns, these fungi were replaced by various species of brittlecap, milky cap, and other death cap fungi. The least conservative boletes and golden chanterelles also began fruiting that year. In 2007, more bolete species, *Boletus submentosus, Boletus griseus, Boletus inedulis,* and *Leccinum nigrescens,* appeared. In 2008 we collected over fifty king boletes, a choice edible, under white oaks just south of the trail. That was also the year the first gilled bolete, *Phylloporus rhodoxanthus,* fruited at Timberhill. The next year, I collected the first *Leccinum subglabripes* in this site.

To understand the changes taking place Timberhill oak savanna I always carry a small writing pad where I note field observations. Since 2005 I have recorded each mushroom observation including plant associates, substrate, and whether the mushrooms were scattered, clustered, or growing singly. The daily accounts were then entered into a permanent field journal. A separate file listed the date, number of specimens, and location of every species. This data has enabled me to chart the progression of ECM fungi from least to most conservative (species dependent on high-quality woodlands). I have observed that the most conservative fungi fruit only in sites that support highly conservative plants and concluded that this fungal progression indicates that the land is healing. It has also given me deeper insight into oak savanna ecosystem ecology.

9.

LET NATURE DO ITS WORK

IN A FULLY FUNCTIONING OAK SAVANNA, it is the interactions between the fungi, bacteria, soil microbes, insects, other animals, and plants that will restore the ecosystem and allow it to continue to evolve. From the tiniest microbe to the stateliest oak tree, all of the organisms that comprise the savanna are connected. The foundation of this network remains in the native plants and fungi that have survived (Chaudhary and Griswold 2001). Activated by fire and sunlight, this network will restore itself. Too much human intervention will only retard the process.

The restoration process is too complex and mysterious to be completely understood; we cannot take it back to a laboratory, put it under a microscope, and study it. However, Bill and I have learned to become careful observers of these interactions and monitor changes as they occur. We can study the responses to fire and available sunlight and compute the floristic quality of the plants and fungi, but we have no metric to measure the system as a whole, because no lists of all of the plants, animals, and fungi that comprised pre-settlement oak savannas exist. But we are learning what belongs here as Timberhill continues to evolve and plants, fungi, and animals that have a strong affinity for this system become more dominant.

As a diverse community of conservative forbs gradually replaced the early successional woodland sunflower and tick trefoil in the East Savanna understory, I observed that the two plants lousewort and bastard toadflax often dominated sites where woodland sunflower and tick trefoil were declining. Lousewort and bastard toadflax are both root hemiparasites. They are able to produce their own food through the use of solar energy, but they obtain water and nutrients from a host plant. Roots of hemiparasites attach belowground to the roots of their host, robbing it of water and nutrients. A soil fungus acts as a bridge between the parasite and the host (Nickrent 2002). Stimulated by fire, both of these hemiparasites have become abundant at Timberhill. They attack a wide range of species and alter the plant community structure by starving the host plant of nutrients and opening a site for more conservative plants.

Lousewort and dwarf larkspur blooming in a prairie opening

With its finely cut foliage, lousewort is often mistaken for a fern. In late spring, a dense cluster of small yellow snapdragon-like flowers bloom on top of the stem. Once established, these plants spread like a fairy ring in an ever-widening circle. At the perimeter of the circle, lousewort moves through the border of plants such as

woodland sunflower. At Timberhill we have observed that woodland sunflowers parasitized by lousewort become less vigorous,
growing to half their normal size with fewer than normal flowering
stems. As they decline, space is opened for more conservative forbs.
Inside the circle conservative plants such as slender bush clover and
blazing star replace the woodland sunflower and lousewort, which
disappears completely.

Lousewort outcompeting blackberries in a West 40 briar patch

At Timberhill, lousewort is influencing the plant composition in
several sites. It has completely surrounded a small ridgetop prairie
remnant in the West 40 unit. Working its way downhill through the
adjacent woodland, it reduces the height and density of goldenrod,
woodland sunflower, and big bluestem in its path. There is a distinct
line between the perimeter of the lousewort and the taller plants in
the remnant prairie. Lousewort has also changed the plant composition on several oak ridges in the East Savanna. In the southeast corner,
it has moved across the trail that dissects the woodland on the last

ridge. This site has taken ten years to progress from successional stage 1 to stage 2. Lousewort is now leading the way to stage 3 as it expands its circle of dominance.

Bastard toadflax

I first noticed bastard toadflax on top of the open ridge where we began our savanna restoration. Bastard toadflax is easy to overlook with its short stem of narrow alternate leaves and small white, star-shaped flowers. The long, slender suckers of the rootstocks parasitize asters, goldenrod, pussytoes, and sedges (Moss 1926). In the East Savanna, bastard toadflax has paved the way for scaly blazing star and cream wild indigo. Before restoration, the remnant populations of these plants were very sparse. They have now spread throughout the ridgetop along with many other highly conservative wildflowers. Unlike lousewort, bastard toadflax continues to work both within a community of plants such as those on the open ridge and in more densely wooded sites dominated by woodland sunflower. It does not disappear.

Bastard toadflax working in a prairie opening

Orange dodder, another type of parasitic plant, is changing the plant composition in a riparian area along Brush Creek. Dodder is a holoparasite and cannot produce its own carbohydrates; it is totally reliant on its host for survival. In the Brush Creek riparian area, it is spreading through the tall stalks of wingstem, weakening it and reducing its dominance. An understory of short grasses and sedges is replacing the wingstem.

Orange dodder, a holoparasite

One cannot understate the importance of soil fungi (arbuscular mycorrhizas, or AM fungi) in the ecosystem. These fungi do not produce mushrooms. They attach to the roots of mycorrhizal-dependent plants, extending the plants' ability to capture water and nutrients. The AM fungi provide native plants with inorganic nutrients such as phosphorus and nitrogen in exchange for sugar from the plants (Stamets 2005). (Fungi cannot produce their own sugar.)

This mutually beneficial relationship between the fungi and mycorrhizal-dependent plants favors conservative native plants. Native plants evolved with the fungi and have a high mycorrhizal dependency. The AM fungi in a site are ones that will increase the growth and vigor of plants that belong in that site. AM fungi are beneficial to conservative native plants and harmful to invasive weeds and nonnative plants. Mycorrhizal-dependent plants outcompete nonmycorrhizal plants because of the nutrients supplied to them by the fungi. The fungi also enhance the number of species that can coexist in a site because so many more nutrients are available to the plants.

Natural soil communities contain a wide variety of these fungi. Disturbing the soil by grazing or tilling suppresses the fungi and will eventually destroy them (Chaudhary and Griswold 2001). On the other hand, AM fungi are stimulated by an abundance of native plants and the availability of nutrients from dead plant material. The more vegetative matter there is to break down, the more soil fungi will respond.

Natural processes are also increasing the oak dominance at Timberhill. The hickory grove in the West 40 unit was a pure stand of shagbark hickory after we first thinned it in 2002. Since then, fire (hickories are not as fire tolerant as oaks) and storm loss have reduced the hickory population and stimulated white and black oak reproduction. Young oak trees are now becoming established in the grove and will eventually replace the hickory. They are even moving into a prairie opening to the north, replicating the transitional zone between eastern deciduous woodlands and the tallgrass prairie. Historically this zone was never constant, as it metamorphosed from open prairie to savanna in response to fire and drought.

Young white oaks moving into a prairie opening

Bur oaks are also moving into the West Creek prairie remnants. Before 1965, most of this unit had been prairie-pasture. The grazing stopped after the creek cut too deeply to maintain a fence across the water gap. Honey locust, eastern red cedar, and elms then spread throughout the prairie-pastureland. When we purchased it, dense clusters of eastern red cedar had invaded the open land and honey locusts dominated the riparian area. Beginning in 2005 after three annual burns, we cut down all the trees except the elms. (Elms are highly susceptible to Dutch elm disease. As they die, highly prized morel mushrooms often fruit from the base of the dead and dying trees.) Continued prescribed fire and thinning restored the bunch grass, sedge, and prairie wildflower dominance in this unit. And now we are observing the next stage of the natural processes, as fire-resistant bur oaks are becoming established in the prairie.

The pioneer spring, located on the second rise above the creek in the West Creek unit, is near the site of the original settlers' cabin. These earliest settlers drew all of their water from the spring. According to the previous owner, the spring supplied abundant water even in drought. It was still active when we purchased West Creek, but the water flow had decreased substantially. The prairie-remnant hillside above the spring had become overgrown with weed trees, and precipitation that would have been absorbed into the soil by prairie grasses and sedges was being by gobbled up by the eastern red cedar or running downhill. After we cut and burned the eastern red cedar and implemented prescribed fire, sedges and warm-season grasses repopulated the hillside. As they increased, the land became stingier and the hillside no longer shed rainwater. We observed that the lines of the hillside were softening as the land slumped to a stable angle of repose associated with the redevelopment of groundwater movement and as water flow to the spring increased.

Visitors to Timberhill often comment that we were fortunate to find such a pristine site, implying that what happened here is not possible elsewhere. But like many other oak savanna remnants, our land had been heavily grazed and deprived of sunlight and fire for decades. It is just a small portion of the twenty thousand acres of highly restorable savanna in Decatur County, Iowa (Jim Munson, personal communication 2005). Thousands of acres being restored in Missouri state parks and preserves have also proved that our land is not unique. They, too, required only fire and sunlight to restore a diverse understory of wildflowers, grasses, and sedges.

Savanna restoration doesn't require a large acreage. A fully functioning oak savanna can be restored on as little as 10 acres (Jim Munson, personal communication 2006). Whatever the size of the plot, the degree of recovery depends on land-use history and how severely and for how long it was degraded. The longer we wait, the less quickly savanna remnants will recover.

Bill and I believe that restoration does not involve human mastery over nature. Instead it is based on direct relationships with the landscape. We have such a primitive understanding of how nature works that we can only observe the natural processes and proceed based on experience guided by instinct. We learn by observation, by intuition, and by connecting with the land. We establish a relationship with the land and become integrated into the whole. As the land heals, the relationships in the community are restored and integrated, rebooting the ecosystem. We are the land's partners, not its masters.

APPENDIX I:

TIMBERHILL PLANT LIST

Acalypha gracilens	slender three-seeded mercury
Acalypha rhomboidea	three-seeded mercury
Acalypha virginica	three-seeded mercury
Acer negundo	box elder
Acer saccharinum	silver maple
ACHILLEA MILLEFOLIUM	common yarrow
Achillea millefolium ssp. lanulosa	western yarrow
Adiantum pedatum	northern maidenhair fern
Aesculus glabra	Ohio buckeye
Agalinis auriculata	eared false foxglove
Agalinis gattingeri	round-stemmed false foxglove
Agalinis tenuifolia	slender false foxglove
Agastache nepetoides	yellow giant hyssop
Agrimonia gryposepala	tall agrimony
Agrimonia parviflora	swamp agrimony
Agrimonia pubescens	soft agrimony
AGROSTIS GIGANTEA	redtop
Agrostic hyemalis	tickle grass
Agrostis perennans	upland grass
AGROSTIS STOLONIFERA var. PLALUSTRIS	creeping bent

Alisma plantago-aquatica	water plantain
Allium canadense	wild onion
Allium tricoccum	wild leek
Alopecurus carolinianus	common foxtail
Ambrosia artemisiifolia	common ragweed
Ambrosia trifida	giant ragweed
Amelanchier arborea	serviceberry
Amorpha canescens	leadplant
Amphicarpaea bracteata	hog peanut
Andropogon gerardii	big bluestem grass
Anemone virginiana	tall anemone
Antennaria neglecta	cat's feet
Antennaria plantaginifolia	pussy toes
Apios americana	groundnut
Apocynum adrosaemifolium	spreading dogbane
Apocynum cannabinum	Indian hemp
Apocynum sibiricum	Indian hemp
Apocynum X medium	hybrid dogbane
Aquilegia canadensis	columbine
Arabis canadensis	sickle pod
Arabis hirsuta	hairy rock cress
Arisaema dracontium	green dragon
Arisaema triphyllum	Jack-in-the-pulpit
Asarum canadense	wild ginger
Asclepias hirtella	tall green milkweed
Asclepias incarnata	swamp milkweed
Asclepias purpurascens	purple milkweed
Asclepias quadrifolia	four-leaf milkweed
Asclepias sullivantii	prairie milkweed
Asclepias syriaca	common milkweed

Asclepias tuberosa	butterfly weed
Asclepias verticillata	whorled milkweed
Asplenium platyneuron	ebony spleenwort
Aster azureus	sky-blue aster
Aster drummondii	Drummond's aster
Aster ericoides	heath aster
Aster laevis	smooth blue aster
Aster lanceolatus	panicled aster
Aster novae-angliae	New England aster
Aster ontarionis	Ontario aster
Aster parviceps	small-headed aster
Aster pilosus	hairy aster
Aster puniceus	swamp aster
Astralagus canadensis	Canadian milk vetch
Athyrium filis-femina var. angustum	northern lady fern
Aureolaria grandiflora var. pulchra	yellow false foxglove
Baptisia bracteata var. glabrescens	cream wild indigo
Baptisia lactea	white wild indigo
BARBAREA VULGARIS	yellow rocket
Betula nigra	river birch
Bidens frondosa	beggar ticks
Bidens poplylepis	bur marigold
Botrychium dissectum var. obliquum	cut-leaved grape fern
Botrychhium virginianum	rattlesnake fern
Brachyelytrum erectum	long-awned wood grass
Brassica kaber	charlock
Bromus pubescens	woodland brome
Cacalia atriplicifolia	Indian plantain
Calamagrostis canadensis	blue joint grass
Calystegia sepium	hedge bindweed

Camassia scilloides	wild hyacinth
Campanula americana	tall bellflower
CAPSELLA BURSA-PASTORIS	shepherd's purse
Cardamine parviflora var. arenicola	small-flowered bitter cress
Carex aggregata	smooth clustered sedge
Carex annectens var. xanthocarpa	large yellow fox sedge
Carex bicknellii	Bicknell's sedge
Carex blanda	common wood sedge
Carex bushii	long-scaled green sedge
Carex cephalopohora	short-headed bracted sedge
Carex cristatella	crested oval sedge
Carex davisii	awned graceful sedge
Carex festucacea	fescue oval sedge
Carex frankii	bristly cattail sedge
Carex gravida	long-awned bracted sedge
Carex grisea	gray sedge
Carex haydenii	long-scaled tussock sedge
Carex hirsutella	hairy green sedge
Carex hirtifolia	hairy wood sedge
Carex jamesii	grass sedge
Carex leavenworthii	dwarf bracted sedge
Carex meadii	Mead's stiff sedge
Carex molesta	field oval sedge
Carex muhlenbergii	sand bracted sedge
Carex normalis	spreading oval sedge
Carex oligocarpa	few-fruited gray sedge
Carex pellita	broad-leaved woolly sedge
Carex pensylvanica	Pennsylvania oak sedge
Carex radiata	straight-styled wood sedge
Carex rosea	curly-styled wood sedge

Carex sparganioides	loose-headed bracted sedge
Carex stricta	common tussock sedge
Carex suberecta	wedge fruited oval sedge
Carex tenera	narrow-leaved oval sedge
Carex tribuloides	awl-fruited oval sedge
Carex vulpinoidea	brown fox sedge
Carya cordiformis	bitternut hickory
Carya ovata	shagbark hickory
Ceanothus americanus var. pitcheri	New Jersey tea
Celastrus scandens	bittersweet
Celtis occidentalis	hackberry
CERASTIUM VULGATUM	mouse-ear chickweed
Chaerophyllum procumbens	chervil
Chamaecrista fasciculata	partridge pea
Chenopodium standleyanum	woodland goosefoot
Cicuta maculata	water hemlock
Cinna arundinacea	wood reed
Circaea lutetiana var. canadensis	enchanter's nightshade
Cirsium altissimum	tall thistle
CIRSIUM ARVENSE	field thistle
Cirsium discolor	pasture thistle
Claytonia virginica	spring beauty
Coeloglossum viride var. virescens	bracted orchid
Comandra umbellata	Bastard toadflax
Conyza canadensis	horseweed
Corallorhiza odontorhiza	fall coral root orchid
Coreopsis palmata	prairie coreopsis
Coreopsis tripteris	tall tickseed
Cornus drummondii	rough-leaved dogwood
Cornus racemosa	gray dogwood

Corylus americana	American hazelnut
Crataegus crus-galli	cockspur hawthorn
Crataegus succulenta	fleshy hawthorn
Cryptotaenia canadensis	honewort
Cuscuta gronovii	common dodder
Cyperus strigosus	long-scaled nut sedge
Cypripedium calceolus var. pubescens	yellow lady's slipper orchid
Cystopteris fragilis	fragile fern
Cystopteris protrusa	Creeping fragile fern
DACTYLIS GLOMERATA	orchard grass
Dalea candida	white prairie clover
Dalea purpurea	purple prairie clover
Danthonia spicata	poverty oat grass
Delphinium tricorne	dwarf larkspur
Dentaria laciniata	toothwort
Desmodium canadense	showy tick trefoil
Desmodium glutinosum	pointed tick trefoil
Desmodiium paniculatum	panicled tick trefoil
DIANTHUS ARMERIA	Deptford pink
Dicentra cucullaria	Dutchman's breeches
DIGITARIA SANGUINALIS	common crabgrass
Dioscorea villosa	wild yam
Echinacea pallida	pale coneflower
Echinacea purpurea	purple coneflower
ECHINOCHLOA CRUSGALLI	barnyard grass
Eleocharis erythropoda	red-rooted spike rush
Eleocharis obtusa	blunt spike rush
Eleocharis tenuis	slender spike rush
Ellisia nyctelea	Aunt Lucy
Elymus riparius	riverbank wild rye

Elymus villosus	slender wild rye
Elymus virginicus	Virginia wild rye
Epilobium coloratum	cinnamon willow herb
Equisetum arvense	common horsetail
Equisetum X ferrissii	hybrid scouring rush
Eragrostis pectinacea	small love grass
Eragrostis spectabilis	purple love grass
Erigeron annuus	annual fleabane
Erigeron strigosus	daisy fleabane
Erygium yuccifolium	rattlesnake master
Erythronium albidum	white trout lily
Eupatorium perfoliatum	boneset
Eupatorium purpureum	purple Joe Pye weed
Eupatorium rugosum	white snakeroot
Eupatorium serotinum	late boneset
Euphorbia corollata	flowering spurge
Euthamia graminifolia	grass-leaved goldenrod
Festuca obtusa	nodding fescue
Fragaria virginiana	wild strawberry
Fraxinus americana	white ash
Fraxinus pennsylvanica	red ash
Fraxinus pennsylvanica var.	
lanceolata	green ash
Galium circaezans	wild licorice
Galium concinnum	shining bedstraw
Galium obtusum	wild madder
Galium triflorum	sweet-scented bedstraw
Gaura biennis	biennial gaura
Gentiana alba	yellowish gentian
Gentiana andrewsii	bottle gentian

Geranium maculatum	wild geranium
Geum canadense	white avens
Geum laciniatum	rough avens
Geum vernum	spring avens
Gleditsia triacanthos	honey locust
Glyceria striata	fowl manna grass
Hackelia virginiana	stickseed
Hedeoma pulegioides	American pennyroyal
Helenium autumnale	sneezeweed
Helianthemum bicknellii	rockrose
Helianthemum canadense	common rockrose
Helianthus divaricatus	woodland sunflower
Helianthus strumosus	pale-leaved sunflower
Heliopsis helianthoides	false sunflower
Heuchera richardsonii	prairie alum root
Hieracium longipilum	hawkweed
Hieraciium scabrum	rough hawkweed
Humulus lupulus	common hops
Hydrophyllum virginianum	Virginia waterleaf
Hypericum mutilum	dwarf St. John's wort
Hypericum punctatum	spotted St. John's wort
Hypoxis hirsuta	yellow star grass
Hystrix patula	bottlebrush grass
Impatiens capensis	spotted touch-me-not
Impatiens pallida	pale touch-me-not
Isopyrum biternatum	false rue anemone
Juglans nigra	black walnut
Juncus interior	inland rush
Juncus tenuis	path rush
Juniperus virginiana	red cedar

Koeleria macrantha	June grass
Krigia biflora	false dandelion
KUMMEROWIA STIPULACEA	Korean clover
Lactuca canadensis	wild lettuce
Lactuca floridana	blue lettuce
LAMIUM AMPLEXICAULE	henbit
Laportea canadensis	wood nettle
Leersia oryzoides	rice cut grass
Leersia virginica	white grass
Lepidium densiflorum	peppercress
Leptoloma cognatum	fall witch grass
Lespedeza capitata	round-headed bush clover
Lespedeza violacea	violet bush clover
Lespedeza virginica	slender bush clover
LEUCANTHEMUM VULGARE	ox-eye daisy
Liatris aspera	rough blazing star
Liatris cylindracea	cylindrical blazing star
Liatris squarrosa	squarrose blazing star
Lilium michiganense	Michigan lily
Linum sulcatum	grooved yellow flax
Liparis liliifolia	purple twayblade
Lithospermum canescens	hoary puccoon
Lobelia inflata	Indian tobacco
Lobelia siphilitica	great blue lobelia
Lobelia spicata	spiked lobelia
LOTUS CORNICULATUS	bird's-foot trefoil
Ludwigia alternifolia	seedbox
Lycopus americanus	common water horehound
Lycopus virginicus	bugleweed
Lysimachia ciliata	fringed loosestrife

Lythrum alatum	winged loosestrife
Malus ioensis	Iowa crab
Mertensia virginica	Virginia bluebells
Mimulus alatus	winged monkey flower
Mimulus ringens	monkey flower
Moehringia lateriflora	wood sandwort
Monarda fistulosa	wild bergamot
Monotropa hypopithus	pinesap
Monotropa uniflora	Indian pipe
MORUS ALBA	white mulberry
Muhlenbergia frondosa	common satin grass
Muhlenbergia schreberi	nimblewill
Muhlenbergia tenuiflora	slender satin grass
Najas quadalupensis	southern naiad
Oenothera biennis	common evening primrose
Onoclea sensibilis	sensitive fern
Osmorhiza claytonia	hairy sweet cicely
Osmorhiza longistylis	smooth sweet cicely
Ostrya virginiana	hop hornbeam
Oxalis dillenii	common wood sorrel
Oxalis stricta	tall wood sorrel
Oxalis violacea	violet wood sorrel
Panicum clandestinum	deer-tongue grass
Panicum implicatum	old-field panic grass
Panicum latifolium	broad-leaved panic grass
Panicum oligosanthes var. scribnerianum	Scribner's panic grass
Panicum perlongum	long-stalked panic grass
Parietaria pensylvanica	pellitory
Parthenium integrifolium	wild quinine

Parthenocissus quinquefolia	Virginia creeper
Paronychia fastigiata	forked chickweed
Paspalum setaceum var. muhlenbergii	hairy lens grass
Pedicularis canadensis	lousewort
Penstemon digitalis	foxglove beardtongue
Penstemon pallidus	pale beardtongue
Penthorum sedoides	ditch stonecrop
PHALARIS ARUNDINACEA	reed canary grass
PHLEUM PRATENSE	Timothy
Phlox divaricata	woodland phlox
Phlox pilosa	prairie phlox
Phryma leptostachya	lopseed
Physalis virginiana	ground cherry
Pilea pumila	common clearweed
Plantago aristata	bracted plantain
Plantago rugelii	red-stalked plantain
Plantago virginica	dwarf plantain
POA COMPRESSA	Canadian bluegrass
POA PRATENSIS	Kentucky bluegrass
Poa wolfii	Wolf's bluegrass
Podophyllum peltatum	May apple
Polemonium reptans	Jacob's ladder
Polygola sanguinea	field milkwort
Polygala verticillata	whorled milkwort
Polygonatum biflorum	Solomon's seal
POLYGONUM PERSICARIA	lady's thumb
Polygonum punctatum	water smartweed
Polygonum sagittatum	tearthumb
Polygonum scandens	climbing false buckwheat
Polygonum tenue	slender knotweed

Polygonum virginianum	jumpseed
Populus deltoides	cottonwood
Potentilla norvegica	Norway cinquefoil
POTENTILLA RECTA	sulphur cinquefoil
Potentilla simplex	common cinquefoil
Prenanthes alba	white lettuce
Prenanthes aspera	rough white lettuce
Prunella vulgaris var. lanceolata	self-heal
Prunus americana	smooth wild plum
Prunus serotina	wild black cherry
Pycnanthemum pilosum	hairy mountain mint
Pycnanthemum tenuifolium	slender mountain mint
Pycnanthemum virginianum	common mountain mint
Quercus alba	white oak
Quercus imbricaria	shingle oak
Quercus macrocarpa	bur oak
Quercus muhlenbergii	chinquapin oak
Quercus rubra	northern red oak
Quercus velutina	black oak
Quercus X bebbiana	Bebb's oak
Quercus X hawkinsiae	Hawkin's' oak
Ranunculus abortivus	small-flowered crowfoot
Ranunculus septentrionallis	swamp buttercup
Ratibida pinnata	gray-headed coneflower
Rhamnus lanceolata	lance-leaved buckthorn
Rhus aromatica	fragrant sumac
Rhus glabra	smooth sumac
Ribes missouriense	wild gooseberry
Rorippa sessilifolia	sessile-flowered cress
Rosa arkansana var. suffulta	sunshine rose

Rosa carolina	pasture rose
ROSA MULTIFLORA	multiflora rose
Rosa setigera	prairie rose
Rubus allegheniensis	common blackberry
Rubus alumus	common blackberry
Rubus curtipes	short-stalked dewberry
Rubus frondosus	blackberry
Rubus meracus	dewberry
Rubus occidentalis	black raspberry
Rubus pensilvanicus	Yankee blackberry
Rubus recurvans	recurved blackberry
Rubus setosis	bristly blackberry
Rubus steelei	Steele's blackberry
Rudbeckia hirta	black-eyed Susan
Rudbeckia laciniata	wild golden glow
Rudbeckia subtomentosa	sweet black-eyed Susan
Rudbeckia triloba	brown-eyed Susan
Ruellia humilis	wild petunia
RUMEX CRIPSPUS	curly dock
Rumex occidentalis	western dock
RUMEX PATIENTIA	patience dock
Sagittaria latifolia	common arrowhead
Salix eriocephala	heart-leaved willow
Salix exigua ssp. Interior	sandbar willow
Salix nigra	black willow
Sambucus canadensis	elderberry
Sanguinaria canadensis	bloodroot
Sanicula canadensis	black snakeroot
Sanicula gregaria	common snakeroot
Sanicula marilandica	black snakeroot

Schizachyrium scoparium	little bluestem
Scirpus atrovirens	dark green rush
Scirpus fluviatilis	river bulrush
Scleria triglomerata	tall nut rush
Scrophularia lanceolata	early figwort
Scrophularia marilandica	late figwort
Scutellaria leonardii	small skullcap
Senecio plattensis	prairie ragwort
SETARIA FABERII	giant foxtail
SETARIA GLAUCA	yellow foxtail
Silene antirrhina	sleepy catchfly
Silene stellata	starry campion
Silphium integrifolium	rosinweed
Silphium laciniatum	compass plant
Silphium perfoliatum	cup plant
Sisyrinchium angustifolium	stout blue-eyed grass
Sisyrinchium campestre	prairie blue-eyed grass
Smilacina racemosa	false Solomon's seal
Smilacina stellata	starry false Solomon's seal
Smilax ecirrharta	upright carrion flower
Smilax hispida	greenbrier
Smilax lasioneura	common carrion flower
Solanum americanum	black nightshade
Solanum carolinense	horse nettle
Solidago altissima	tall goldenrod
Solidago canadensis	tall goldenrod
Solidago gigantea	smooth goldenrod
Solidago missouriensis	Missouri goldenrod
Solidago nemoralis	field goldenrod
Solidago riddellii	Riddell's goldenrod

Solidago speciosa	showy goldenrod
Solidago ulmifolia	elm-leaved goldenrod
Sorghastrum nutans	Indian grass
Spartina pectinata	prairie cordgrass
Sphenopholis obtusata var. major	slender wedge grass
Spiranthes lacera	slender ladies' tresses
Spiranthes magnicamporum	Great Plains ladies' tresses
Sporobolus vaginiflorus	sheathed rush grass
Stachys aspera	rough hedge nettle
Stachys palustris	woundwort
STELLARIA MEDIA	common chickweed
Strophostyles helvola	wild bean
Symphoricarpos orbiculatus	coralberry
Symphyotrichum amethystinus	amethyst aster
Taenidia integerrima	yellow pimpernel
TARAXACUM OFFICINALE	common dandelion
Teucrium canadense	germander
Thalictrum dasycarpum	purple meadow rue
Thalictrum dioicum	early meadow rue
Thalictrum revolutum	waxy meadow rue
Thalictrum thalictroides	rue anemone
Tilia americana	basswood
Toxicodendron radicans	poison ivy
Tradescantia ohiensis	common spiderwort
Tridens flavens	purple top
TRIFLOLIUM HYBRIDUM	alsike clover
TRIFOLIUM PRATENSE	red clover
TRIFOLIIUM REPENS	white clover
Triodanis perfoliata	Venus's looking glass
Triosteum aurantiacum	early horse gentian

Triosteum perfoliatum	late horse gentian
Ulmus americana	American elm
Ulmus rubra	slippery elm
Uvularia grandiflora	bellwort
Veratrum woodii	false hellebore
VERBASCUM THAPSUS	common mullein
Verbena hastata	blue vervain
Verbena stricta	hoary vervain
Verbena urticifolia	white vervain
Verbesina alternifolia	wingstem
Vernonia bladwinii	Baldwin's ironweed
Vernonia gigantea	tall ironweed
VERONICA ARVENSIS	corn speedwell
Veronica peregrina	purslane speedwell
Veronicastrum virginicum	Culver's root
Viola pubescens	downy yellow violet
Viola rafinesquii	wild pansy
Viola sororia	hairy blue violet
Vitis riparia	riverbank grape
Zanthoxylum americanum	prickly ash
Zizia aurea	golden Alexanders

APPENDIX 2:

BIRDS OF TIMBERHILL

American crow
American goldfinch
American redstart
American robin
American woodcock
Baltimore oriole
Barn swallow
Barred owl
Belted kingfisher
Black-and-white warbler
Blue grosbeak
Blue jay
Blue-gray Gnatcatcher
Bob white
Brown thrasher
Brown-headed cowbird
Cape May warbler
Carolina wren
Cedar waxwing
Chestnut-sided warbler
Chipping sparrow
Common grackle
Common nighthawk

Common yellowthroat
Dickcissel
Downy woodpecker
Eastern towhee
Eastern bluebird
Eastern kingbird
Eastern phoebe
Eastern wood peewee
Field sparrow
Ferruginous hawk
Grasshopper sparrow
Gray-cheeked thrush
Great-crested flycatcher
Grey catbird
Hairy woodpecker
Henslow's sparrow
House finch
House wren
Indigo bunting
Kentucky warbler
Lark sparrow
Least flycatcher
Louisiana waterthrush

Mourning dove
Northern cardinal
Northern flicker
Northern mockingbird
Northern shrike (1/2011)
Northern parula warbler
Northern rough-winged swallow
Orchard oriole
Ovenbird
Pileated woodpecker
Red-bellied woodpecker
Red-eyed vireo
Redheaded woodpecker
Red-winged blackbird
Rose-breasted grosbeak
Ruby-throated hummingbird
Scarlet tanager

Song sparrow
Summer tanager
Swainson's thrush
Tennessee warbler
Tree swallow
Tufted titmouse
Turkey vulture
Whippoorwill
White-breasted nuthatch
Wild turkey
Wood thrush
Yellow warbler
Yellow-billed cuckoo
Yellow-breasted chat
Yellow-rumped warbler
Yellow-throated vireo

APPENDIX 3:

TIMBERHILL BOLETE MUSHROOMS

Boletus affinus
Boletus badius
Boletus bicolor
Boletus campestris
Boletus dupainii
Boletus edulis
Boletus erythropus
Boletus griseus
Boletus inedulis
Boletus rhodosanguineus
Boletus rubroflammeus
Boletus spadiceus
Boletus submentosus
Gastroboletus turbinatus

Gyroporus castaneus
Leccinum carpini
Leccinum nigrescens
Leccinum rugosiceps
Leccinum sp. #3
Leccinum subglabripes
Phylloporus rhodoxanthus americanus
Strobilomyces floccopus
Tylopilus felleus
Tylopilus plumboviolaceus
Tylopilus rubrobrunneus
Tylopilus sordidus

APPENDIX 4: RESOURCES

Conservation Organizations

Lady Bird Johnson Wildflower Center National Organizations Directory lists native plant societies, conservation groups, governmental agencies, botanical gardens, arboreta, and other plant-related organizations throughout North America. http://www.wildflower.org/organizations/.

Southern Iowa Oak Savanna Alliance provides oak savanna restoration and prescribed fire workshops for landowners. http://www.siosa.org/

The Nature Conservancy
http://www.nature.org/

U.S. Fish & Wildlife Service Partners for Fish & Wildlife
Working with private conservation organizations, state, federal, and tribal agencies, the Partners for Fish & Wildlife program assists private landowners in restoring their properties.
http://www.fws.gov/midwest/partners/

Prescribed Fire Information and Training

Coalition of Prescribed Fire Councils, Inc. assists fire practitioners, policymakers, regulators, and citizens with issues surrounding prescribed fire use.

http://www.prescribedfire.net/.
Fire Learning Network sponsors workshops and exchanges of information in the use of prescribed fire.
http://www.conservationgateway.org/ConservationPractices/FireLandscapes/FireLearningNetwork/Pages/fire-learning-network.aspx

Great Plains Fire Science Exchange, part of the *Joint Fire Science Program,* disseminates grassland and savanna fire information to landowners, managers, practitioners and scientists. This organization also sponsors fire workshops and conferences.
http://gpfirescience.missouristate.edu/default.aspx

National Wildland Fire Training lists courses, workshops, and meetings related to the use of prescribed fire.
http://www.nationalfiretraining.net.

Natural History Education
Eagle Hill Institute offers natural history science and ecological restoration seminars, courses and workshops.
http://www.eaglehill.us/programs/nhs/nhs-calendar.shtml.

Iowa Lakeside Laboratory, an Iowa regents campus located on the shore of Lake Okoboji in northwestern Iowa, offers natural science and ecology classes.
http://www.continuetolearn.uiowa.edu/lakesidelab/index.html

North American Mycological Association promotes scientific and educational activities related to fungi. This organization sponsors regional and national mushroom forays open to the public. A list of affiliated clubs is available on the NAMA website.
http://namyco.org

BIBLIOGRAPHY

Anderson, Roger C., James S. Fralish, and Jerry M. Baskin eds. *Savannas, Barrens, and Rock Outcrop Plant Communities of North America*. Cambridge: Cambridge University Press, 1999.

"More Than One-quarter of United States Birds Need Urgent Conservation Action", *Audubon* website, published November 28, 2007, http://www.audubon.org/newsroom/press-releases/2007/more-one-quarter-united-states-birds-need-urgent-conservation-action.

Aubrey, Keith B. and Catherine M. Raley. "The Pileated Woodpecker as a Keystone Habitat Modifier in the Pacific Northwest." *USDA Forest Service General Technical Reports PSW-GTR-181* (2002): 257–274.

Bardgett, Richard D., Roger S. Smith, Robert S. Shiel, Simon Peacock, Janet M. Simkin, Helen Quirk, and Phil J. Hobbs. "Parasitic Plants Indirectly Regulate Below-ground Properties in Grassland Ecosystems." *Nature* 439 (2006): 969–972.

Bessette, Alan E., William C. Roody, and Arleen R. Bessette. *North American Boletes*. Syracruse: Syracruse University Press, 2000.

Both, Ernst E. *The Boletes of North America*. Buffalo: Buffalo Museum of Science, 1993.

Brawn, Jeffrey D. "Effects of Oak Savanna Restoration on Avian Populations and Communities in Illinois." *Illinois Natural History Survey.* University of Illinois, 1998. https://www.ideals.illinois.edu/bitstream/handle/2142/10484/inhsc-wev01998i0000a_opt.pdf?sequence=2.

Brawn, Jeffrey D., Scott K. Robinson, and Frank R. T. Thompson III. "The Role of Disturbance in the Ecology and Conservation of Birds." *Annual Review of Ecology and Systematics* 32 (2001): 251–276. http://www.annualreviews.org/doi/abs/10.1146/annurev. ecolsys.32.081501.114031.

Bruns, Thomas D. "Thoughts on the Processes that Maintain Local Species Diversity of Ectomycorrhizal Fungi." *Plant Soil* 170 (1995): 63–73.

Brudvig, Lars, and Catherine M. Mabry. "Trait-Based Filtering of the Regional Species Pool to Guide Understory Plant Reintroductions in Midwestern Oak Savannas, U.S.A." *Restoration Ecology* 16 (2008): 290–304.

Cayete, Gregory. *Native Science: Natural Laws of Interdependence.* Santa Fe: Clear Light Publishers, 2000.

Chaudhary, Bala and Margot Griswold. "Mycorrhizal Fungi: A Restoration Practitioner's Point of View." *Ecesis* 12. California Society for Ecological Restoration (2001), http://www.newfieldsrestoration.com/PDFs/Mycorrhizal_Fungi_ Ecesis.pdf.

Cilimburg, A. C. and Karen Short. "Forest Fire in the Northern Rockies: A Primer" (2005), accessed December 28, 2012. http://www.northernrockiesfire.org.

Clark, J. S. and P. D. Royal. "Transformation of a Northern Hardwood Forest by Aboriginal(Iroquios) Fire: Charcoal Evidence from Crawford Lake, Ontario, Canada." *The Holocene* 5, no.1 (1995): 1-9. http://labs.eeb.utoronto.ca/mcandrews/PDFs/Laboratory/Transformationhardwoodfire.pdf.

Curtis, John T. *The Vegetation of Wisconsin.* Madison: University of Wisconsin Press, 1959.

Davis, Mark A., David W. Richardson, Peter B. Reich, Michelle Crozier, Toby Query, Eliot Mitchell, Josh Huntington, and Paul Bazakas. "Restoring Savanna Using Fire: Impact on the Breeding Bird Community." *Restoration Ecology* 8, no. 2 (2000): 30–40.

Debinski, D. and A. Babbitt. "Butterfly Species in Native Prairies and Restored Prairie." *Prairie Naturalist* 29 (1997): 219–227.

Delong, Karl T. and Craig Hooper. "A Potential Understory Flora for Oak Savanna in Iowa." *Journal of the Iowa Academy of Science* 103 (1996): 9–98.

DeSantis, Ryan D., Stephen W. Hallgren, and David W. Stahle. "Historic Fire Regime of an Upland Oak Forest in South-Central North America." *Fire Ecology* 6 (2010): 45–61.

Dickie, Ian A., Rebecca C. Guza, Sarah E. Krazewski, and Peter B. Reich. "Shared Ectomycorrhizal Fungi between a Herbaceous Perennial (*Helianthemum bicknellii*) and Oak (*Quercus*) Seedlings." *New Phytologist* 164 (2004): 375–382.

Dighton, John. *Fungi in Ecosystem Processes*. New York: Marcel Dekker, 2003.

Dudley, Nigel and Daniel Vallaurt. "Deadwood—Living Forests." *World Wildlife Fund Report*, 2004.
http://wwf.panda.org/about_our_earth/all_publications/?15899/Deadwood-living-forests-The-importance-of-veteran-trees-and-deadwood-to-biodiversity.

"How Coyote Brought Fire to the People: A Karok(Karuk) Legend", *First People*, accessed December 28, 2012 htpp://www.firstpeople.us.

Fitzpatrick, T. J. and M. F. L. Fitzpatrick. Flora of Southern Iowa." *Iowa Academy of Science* 5 (1898): 137–178.

Fitzpatrick T. J. and M. F. L. Fitzpatrick. "Flora of Southern Iowa. II." *Iowa Academy of Science* 6 (1899): 173–202.

Fitzpatrick, T. J. and M. F. L. Fitzpatrick. "Native Oak Grove of Iowa." *The Plant World* IV (1901): 69–71.

Fralish, James S. "The Central Hardwood Forest: Its Boundaries and Physiographic Provinces." *USDA Forest Service, General Technical Reports SRS-73* (2003): 78–87.
http://www.woodweb.com/knowledge_base/fpl_pdfs/CHvolume13page001.pdf.

Fralish, James S. "The Keystone Role of Oak and Hickory in the Central Hardwood Forest." USDA Forest Service, *General Technical Reports SRS-73* (2004): 78–87.

Groninger, John. W., Leslie A. Horner, John L. Nelson, and Charles M. Ruffner. "Prescribed Fire and Oak Ecosystem Maintenance: A Primer for Land Managers." Carbondale: Department of Forestry Southern Illinois University, 2005.

Forest Enterprise. *Life in the* Deadwood. Edinburgh: Forest Enterprise—Environment and Communications, 2002. http://www. forestry.gov.uk/pdf/lifeinthedeadwood.pdf/$FILE/lifeinthedeadwood. pdf.

Hartman, George W. "Forest Land Management Guide: Use of Prescribed Fire." Missouri Department of Conservation (2005). http://www.arfirenetwork.org/cms/docs/mo_fire_mgmt_man.pdf.

Hedberg, Andrew M., Victoria A. Borowicz, and Joseph E. Armstrong. "Interactions between a Hemiparasitic Plant *Pedicularis canadensis* (*Scrophulariaceae*) and Members of a Tallgrass Prairie Community." *Journal of the Torrey Botanical Society* 132, no. 3 (2005): 401–410.

Henderson, Richard. "Are There Keystone Plant Species Driving Diversity in Midwest Prairies?" *Proceedings of 18th North American Prairie Conference* (2002): 63–66. Truman State University Press.

Henkes, Rollie. "Timberhill and the Education of Sibylla and Bill Brown." *Woodlands and Prairies Magazine,*8,no. 3 (2011):4-12.

Higgens, Kenneth F., Arnold D. Kruse, and James L. Piehl. *Prescribed Burning Guidelines in the Northern Great Plains*. US Fish and Wildlife Service: EC 700, 1989.

Howell, J. M. and Heman C. Smith. *History of Decatur County and Its People*. Chicago: Clarke Publishing, 1915.

Jonsson, Lena. "Community Structure of Ectomycorrhizal Fungi in Swedish Boreal Forests." Northern Ireland Fungus Group website (1998).
http://www.nifg.org.uk/ecto.htm.

Kaufman, Kenn. *Lives of North American Birds*. New York: Houghton Mifflin, 1996.

McCarthy, Brian C. and Scott A. Robinson. "Canopy Openness, Understory Light Environments, and Oak Regeneration." *US Forest Service General Technical Reports NE-299* (2003): 62.
http://www.fs.fed.us/ne/newtown_square/publications/technical_reports/pdfs/2003/gtrne299.pdf.

McCarty, Ken. "Landscape-Scale Restoration in Missouri Savannas and Woodlands." *Restoration and Management Notes* 16, no. 1 (1998): 22–32.

McPherson, Guy R. *Ecology and Management of North American Savannas*. Tucson: University of Arizona Press, 1997.

Moss, E. H. "Parasitism in the Genus Comandra." *New Phytologist* 24 (1926): 264–276.

National Resources Conservation Service. "Prescribed Burning." *Iowa Job Sheet: Conservation Practice* 338, 2009.

Nickrent, Daniel L. "Parasitic Plants of the World." In *Parasitic Plants of the Iberian Peninsula and Balearic Islands*, edited by J. A. Lopez-Saez, P. Catalan, and L. Saez, 7–27. Madrid: Mundi-Prensa, 2002. http://www.plantbiology.siu.edu/faculty/nickrent/NickrentPDFs/Chapter2.pdf.

Nuzzo, Victoria A. "Extent and Status of Midwest Oak Savanna: Presettlement and 1985." *Natural Areas Journal* 6 (1986): 6–36.

Phillips, Ross, Todd Hutchinson, Lucy Brudnak, and Thomas Waldrop. "Fire and Fire Surrogate Treatments in Mixed-Oak Forest: Effects on Herbaceous Layer Vegetation." *USDA Forest Service Proceedings RMRS-P-46* (2007). http://www.treesearch.fs.fed.us/pubs/28592.

Pyne, Stephen J. *Fire in America*. Seattle: University of Washington Press, 1982.

Pruka, Brian W. "Indicator Plants Species of Recoverable Oak Savannas and Open Oak Woodlands in Southern Wisconsin 1995." *1995 Midwest Oak Savanna and Woodland Ecosystems Conferences*, 1995 http://www.epa.gov/ecopage/upland/oak/oak95/app-e.htm.

Ramsbottom, John. *Mushrooms and Toadstools*. London: Collins, 1953.

Ricketts, Taylor H., Eric Dinerstein, David M. Olson, Colby J. Loucks. *Terrestrial Ecoregions of North America: A Conservation Assessment.* Covelo: Island Press (1999).

"The Red-headed Woodpecker." Red-headed Woodpecker Recovery website (2007).
http://www.redheadrecovery.org/index.html.

Robinson S., Terry Cook, Steve Chaplin, and Eric Dinerstein. "Central Forest-Grasslands Transition." *World Wildlife Fund* (2001).
http://worldwildlife.org/ecoregions/na0804.

Shimek, B. "Prairie Openings in the Forest." *Iowa Academy of Sciences* 17 (1910): 16–19

Sibley, David Allen. *The Sibley Guide to Bird Life and Behavior*. New York: Alfred A. Knopf, 2001.

Smith, Alexander M. and Harry D. Thiers. *The Boletes of Michigan*. Ann Arbor: University of Michigan Press, 1971.

Smith, Sally E. and David Read. *Mycorrhizal Symbiosis*. 3rd ed. Amsterdam: Elsevier, 2009.

Spooner, Brian and Peter Roberts. *Fungi*. London: Collins New Naturalist Library, 2005.

Stamets, Paul. *Mycelium Running*. Berkley: Ten Speed Press, 2005.

Stein, John, Denise Binion, and Robert Aciavatti. *Field Guide to Native Oak Species of Eastern North America*. Morgantown: United States Department of Agriculture Forest Service (2003).

Steyermark, Julian A. *Flora of Missouri*. Ames: Iowa State University Press (1963).

Stewart, Omer C. *Forgotten Fires. Native Americans and the Transient Wilderness*. Norman: University of Oklahoma Press (2002).

Swink, Floyd, and Gerould Wilhelm. *Plants of the Chicago Region*. 4th ed. Indianapolis: Indiana Academy of Science, 1994.

Tallamy, Douglas W. *Bringing Nature Home*. Portland: Timber Press, 2009.

Tedersoo, Leho, Triin Suvi, Ellen Larsson, and Urmas Koljalg. "Diversity and Community Structure of Ectomycorrhizal Fungi in a Wooded Meadow." *Mycological Research* 100 (2006): 734–748

US Environmental Protection Agency. "1995 Midwest Oak Savanna and Woodland Ecosystems Conferences" (1995). http://www.epa.gov/ecopage/upland/oak/oak95/app-a.htm.

Urbrock, William J. ed. "Overview of Midwestern Oak Savanna." *Transactions of the Wisconsin Academy of Sciences, Arts and Letters* 86 (1998): 1-19

Van Bruggen, Theodore. "The Flora of South Central Iowa." Ph.D. diss., University of Iowa, 1958. (available through inter-library loan from the University of Iowa Library)

Van der Heijden, Marcel G. A. and Ian R. Sanders, eds. *Mycorrhizal Ecology*. Berlin: Springer, 2002.

Van der Heijden, Marcel G. A., John N. Klironomos, Margot Ursic, Peter Moutoglis, Ruth Streitworl-Engel, Thomas Boller, Andres Wiemken, and Ian R. Sanders. "Mycorrhizal Fungal Diversity Determines Plant Biodiversity, Ecosystem Variability and Productivity." *Nature* 396 (1998): 69–71.

Veen, C. F., John M. Blair, Melinda D. Smith, and Scott L. Collins. "Influence of Grazing and Fire Frequency on Small-Scale Plant Community Structure and Resource Variability in Native Tall Grass Prairie." *Oikos* 117 (2008): 859–866. http://www.k-state.edu/biology/faculty_pages/blair/Veen et al. Oikos 2008.pdf.

Weir, John W. *Conducting Prescribed Fires: A Comprehensive Guide*. College Station: Texas A&M University Press, 2009.

White, Alan S. "Prescribed Burning for Oak Savanna Restoration in Central Minnesota." *US Department of Agriculture, Forest Service, North Central Forest Experiment Station, Research Paper NC-266* (1986).

Wilhelm, Gerould S. "The Arboretum's East Woods: Are They Lost Forever?" *Morton Arboretum Quarterly* 23 (1987): 54–62.

Wilhelm, Gerould S. and Laura Rericha. *Timberhill Savanna Assessment of Landscape Management*. Williamsburg: Iowa Valley Resource Conservation and Development, 2007. http://www.timberhilloaksavanna.com/TimberhillFinalReport.pdf.

Wisconsin Board of Commissioners of Public Lands. "Wisconsin Public Land Survey Records: Original Field Notes and Plat Maps." http://digicoll.library.wisc.edu/SurveyNotes/SurveyNotesHome.html.

32715780R00079

Made in the USA
Lexington, KY
30 May 2014